MANDARIN
FOOD AND COOKING

MANDARIN
FOOD AND COOKING
75 regional recipes from Beijing and Northern China

TERRY TAN

PHOTOGRAPHY BY MARTIN BRIGDALE

aquamarine

This edition is published by Aquamarine, an imprint of Anness Publishing Ltd, Blaby Road, Wigston, Leicestershire LE18 4SE

info@anness.com

www.aquamarinebooks.com;
www.annesspublishing.com

If you like the images in this book and would like to investigate using them for publishing, promotions or advertising, please visit our website www.practicalpictures.com for more information.

Publisher: Joanna Lorenz
Project Editor: Kate Eddison
Text Editors: Jan Cutler and Catherine Best
Photography: Martin Brigdale
Food Stylist: Katie Giovanni
Prop Stylist: Martin Brigdale
Designer: Simon Daley
Illustrator: Rob Highton
Production Controller: Mai-Ling Collyer

© Anness Publishing Ltd 2013

A CIP catalogue record for this book is available from the British Library.

Publisher's Note

Although the advice and information in this book are believed to be accurate and true at the time of going to press, neither the authors nor the publisher can accept any legal responsibility or liability for any errors or omissions that may have been made, nor for any inaccuracies nor for any loss, harm or injury that comes about from following instructions or advice in this book.

Notes

• Bracketed terms are intended for American readers.
• For all recipes, quantities are given in both metric and imperial measures and, where appropriate, in standard cups and spoons. Follow one set of measures, but not a mixture, because they are not interchangeable.

• Standard spoon and cup measures are level. 1 tsp = 5ml, 1 tbsp = 15ml, 1 cup = 250ml/8fl oz.
• Australian standard tablespoons are 20ml. Australian readers should use 3 tsp in place of 1 tbsp for measuring small quantities.
• American pints are 16fl oz/2 cups. American readers should use 20fl oz/2.5 cups in place of 1 pint when measuring liquids.
• Electric oven temperatures in this book are for conventional ovens. When using a fan oven, the temperature will probably need to be reduced by about 10–20°C/ 20–40°F. Since ovens vary, check with your manufacturer's instruction book for guidance.
• The nutritional analysis given for each recipe is calculated per portion (i.e. serving or item), unless otherwise stated. If the recipe gives a range, such as Serves 4–6, then the nutritional analysis will be for the smaller portion size, i.e. 6 servings. The analysis does not include optional ingredients, such as salt added to taste.
• Medium (US large) eggs are used unless otherwise stated in the text.

Front cover shows Peking Duck – for recipe, see page 84.

Contents

Geography and climate	6
History	8
Cuisine	10
Festivals and celebrations	12
Tools and equipment	14
Classic ingredients	16
Soups and dim sum	22
Fish and shellfish	46
Poultry	66
Meat	86
Pancakes, bread and noodles	108
Vegetables, nuts, eggs and tofu	124
Sweet things	144
Suppliers	156
Index	158

Geography and climate

The expansive land mass of North China stretches from Heilongjiang province in the far north, which borders Russia, all the way to Shanxi province in central China. Bustling, modern Beijing is the heart of this region, being both the cultural and culinary capital. This book focuses on the Beijing school of cooking, as well as on the traditional food of the surrounding area: Hebei, Tianjin, Henan, Shanxi, Shandong, Liaoning, Jilin and Heilongjiang. This northern area is unified by an unforgiving climate and landscape, which has shaped the cuisine.

The undulating landscape of China's northern provinces is varied and impressive, comprising grasslands, rivers, mountains and forests. It is an important agricultural area, feeding a huge population (much of which is clustered in and around the municipality of Beijing), but there are still remote and inhospitable lands in the far north of this vast region.

Topography of Northern China
The valleys, hills and mountains are blanketed metres deep in a fine-grained soil known as loess, a pale mixture of clay and silt deposited by strong winds during the last Ice Age. This fertile substance makes the region a farming heartland.

The northeastern part of this region, containing Heilongjiang, Jilin and Liaoning, is covered with vast forests full of tall pines and cedars, dense bamboos and flamboyant rhododendrons. Between the fields and woodlands lie plateaux that are deeply incised by gorges and ravines

Right Mandarin cuisine uses a mixture of ingredients from the terrains of Manchuria, the Yellow River and the Yellow Sea.
Above Although landlocked, Beijing's cuisine is influenced by the coastlines of Liaoning, Tianjin and Shandong, meaning that fish dishes are plentiful.

containing rushing rivers. Further south, on the densely populated North China Plain, the land becomes flat, with fields of grain stretching for miles.

Farming lands

Wheat is grown in most parts of China, most particularly on the North China Plain (which covers parts of Hebei and Shandong, and is formed from deposits from the Yellow River) and in the Fen River valley in Shanxi. Other grains include corn, millet and oats. The diet of the northern Chinese people has been shaped by local agriculture, and their staple foods are bread and noodles made from these grains. Rice is not grown here.

The influence of the Yellow River

Named for the large quantities of yellowish silt deposited along its banks and in its waters, the famous Yellow River begins in Qinghai in the north-west, flows through many provinces, and empties into the Bo Hai Basin north of the Shandong Peninsula. It runs for an amazing 4,700km (2,940 miles), and has been the cause of many catastrophic floods throughout China's history. Despite

this, the Yellow River is also known as the 'Mother River' of China and the 'cradle of Chinese civilization'. The agricultural areas of Shandong and Henan provinces are irrigated by the Yellow River on its way to the sea. The river also forms the border of Shanxi province, whose central valley is its economic heart, with rich farmlands and flourishing livestock. This area is also steeped in history, and the many temples and monasteries are a reminder that this province was once the political and cultural pulse of China.

Further north lies the historical area of Manchuria, which comprises the modern provinces of Heilongjiang, Liaoning and Jilin, as well as some of Inner Mongolia. Its varied landscape ranges from bustling seaports to vast expanses of uninhabited land unsuited to agriculture. These areas contain towering rock formations, volcanic lakes and dense forests.

The capital city and Hebei

Beijing municipality (formerly known as Peking), the national capital, is carved out of Hebei province, which is largely a farming and industrial area. Beijing is a magnet for tourists, and millions of people

Above **Waterfalls form the spectacular scenery along the waterways of Shanxi.** *Above left* **The Great Wall of China is today a huge tourist attraction.**

visit each year to see the Forbidden City, the Great Wall and Tiananmen Square, and to enjoy the culinary delicacies. Within the city, the ancient settlements of Hutong – a maze of alleyways with distinctive courtyards – sit alongside today's modern flyovers and handsome boulevards.

An extreme climate

The climate in much of northern China is harsh and unforgiving. Summers can reach a scorching 45°C/113°F, while winter temperatures fall to -20°C/-4°F, with bitterly cold winds coursing through from the Mongolian steppes. The growing season diminishes the further north you go; in Manchuria there are only 90 frost-free days per year. The old saying that the northern Chinese will eat 'anything with legs, except a table; and anything that flies, except an aeroplane' refers to the inventiveness of the cuisine, which makes the best of whatever can be grown in the difficult climate.

History

The history of the northern provinces in China is a long and fascinating one. Although theoretically part of North China, the remote, sparsely populated areas of Xinjiang, Tibet and Qinghai have had little influence on the evolution of present-day China. On the other hand, Beijing and the surrounding northern provinces, with their more benign climates and burgeoning populations, have become the powerhouse of Chinese progress in diverse areas – cuisine, politics, the arts, agriculture and industry.

The earliest known settlements, built around 8000BC, were largely primitive villages based on an agricultural economy, and found in the coastal regions of the Shandong peninsula and along the rich deltas of the Yangtze River. The people were hunter-gatherers and fishermen. Archaeological sites in Henan have yielded evidence of carnivore diets, such as fossilized pork bones, that millet, wheat, barley and rice were grown, and that these grains were also turned into alcoholic beverages such as rice wine. Soy beans have been cultivated for more than 3,000 years, and products such as tofu and soy sauce were developed many centuries ago.

The development of the capital city

The emergence of the Song Dynasty in the 10th century saw a period of astounding social, political and culinary advancement. A new middle class emerged, with a consequent increase in demand for the finest materials, food and drink. The sprawling capital city became the domain of the seat of power. Today, Beijing still hosts a wealth of awe-inspiring dynastic sites from centuries ago.

The influence of Mongols and Muslims

By the time of the powerful Mongol leader Genghis Khan in the 13th century, Mongol influences were strong in northern Chinese cuisine. From the earliest times, traditional Mongolian cuisine relied primarily on dairy products and meat. These nomadic people sustained their lives directly from the products of their work animals: horses, cattle, yaks, camels, sheep and goats. Milk, cream, cheese and mutton were important in their diet, and their favourite beverage was fermented mare's milk.

Meanwhile, Chinese Muslims were settling in the region. These settlers came mostly from the Hui, the Uyghur and the

*Below left **This famous Pagoda Forest is located in Henan, at the Shaolin Temple.** Below **A water-filled moat surrounds the Forbidden City in Beijing.***

Above A statue of Chairman Mao stands in Zhongshan Square in Shenyang, the capital city of Liaoning province.

Mongolian minority tribes. As Muslims, they do not eat pork, and therefore lamb, beef and mutton historically made up their diet, and still do today. Hand-made noodles also originated among the Hui, who passed the skills on to imperial chefs, and these skills in turn filtered down to the general populace by the time of the late Qing Dynasty in the 19th century.

China opens up to the world

The 15th century saw China's emergence as a maritime power, and trade links were forged with other nations. Many foreign ingredients were brought back by seafarers and incorporated in the local cuisine. The Portuguese brought chilli peppers, which were embraced with relish, especially towards the western areas. The construction of the Grand Canal in the 17th century facilitated the transportation of rice from the south.

The excesses of the Qing Dynasty

The Qing Dynasty, China's last dynasty, was founded by Nurhachi, and lasted nearly 300 years, from 1644 to 1912. As the first Qing Emperor, Nurhachi unified the scattered tribes of the north, and, under his rule, the Manchus and the Chinese were able to work peacefully together while maintaining their own distinct cultural traditions.

The end of the Qing Dynasty in the 19th century was a turbulent period in Chinese history, with many uprisings. One of the most interesting characters was the ruthless Empress Dowager Cixi (1835–1908). Her epicurean demands famously bordered on the obscene – she lived in such fear that she would be killed, she demanded that meals consist of up to 100 dishes, on the premise that it would have been difficult for someone to poison every dish! An appreciation for the art of cooking, eating and drinking tea became part of everyday Chinese life.

Below The famous Empress Dowager Cixi is pictured with 7 ladies-in-waiting, a child and eunuch attendant.

North China in modern times

The Qing Dynasty was overthrown in the early 20th century and a republic was created. Radical thinking would dominate Chinese history from now until the demise of Chairman Mao. He had reorganized the Communist Party of China (CPC) and initiated the Long March. After the Sino-Japanese War, during World War II, the CPC occupied most of the country from 1949 onwards.

By the end of the 20th century and into the 21st century, the People's Republic of China had changed the way Chinese people thought about their culture and history. There was much social, cultural, land and economic reform. By 1970, most Western nations had established diplomatic ties with the republic.

Beijing is now one of the world's largest cities and the centre of China's political, cultural and culinary culture. China looks set to become the largest and most industrialized economy in the world, with Beijing at its heart. It is developing by looking outwards to other countries while preserving its own culinary and agricultural traditions.

Cuisine

Chinese regional cooking can be said to fall into four categories that roughly correspond to the four points of the compass: north, south, east and west. However, since it is in the nature of cooks to enjoy sharing ideas and recipes, these distinctions are not clear-cut. The northern school of Chinese cuisine is often termed Mandarin cuisine or Beijing-style cooking. Each individual province has its own food history and collection of recipes, but they have influenced each other for many centuries, with similar ingredients dotting the menus.

A Tang Dynasty official once said, "There is nothing that cannot be eaten. Making things edible is only a question of skilfully blending sweet, sour, bitter, salty and peppery flavours while cooking." He was said to have stewed an old saddle and declared it very tasty. Apocryphal perhaps, but the story certainly sums up Chinese attitudes to food.

Beijing cuisine

The focus of northern Chinese cuisine is, of course, the Beijing school. Due to its imperial heritage of excess and affluence, Beijing cuisine came to be regarded as the most sophisticated yet robust style, using simple ingredients in an elaborate way. The elegance of Beijing cooking may

not be apparent to the uninitiated; its simplicity masks clever techniques and a close understanding of the best produce of the region. Beijing cuisine is more influenced by the vast hinterland of Mongolia and beyond than it is by the sea on its eastern shores. Menus are thus rich in lamb, game and poultry, roasted or barbecued to tender perfection, as well as some fresh fish and shellfish from the ocean and rivers.

During the Manchu Dynasty, some 2,000 chefs were employed in the palace kitchens of the Forbidden City. The kitchens were divided into separate departments to make special food for picnics and travelling (emperors journeyed far and wide surveying their

kingdom), and dawn and dusk sacrifices (Taoism and ancestor worship ruled the Chinese household), as well as having divisions just for rice and noodles, pickles and so on. Modern Beijing chefs are proud of their traditional hand-tossed noodles, and in the streets of Beijing you can still see noodle sellers dexterously balancing lumps of dough in their hands, kneading and transforming them into noodles before your eyes.

Below left Cattle and sheep graze on the verdant plains of Hebei province, just outside the municipality of Beijing.
Below Farmers harvest a successful crop of wheat in the fertile countryside of Shandong province.

Above *A fisherman uses traditional methods to break the ice on a frozen lake in Heilongjiang province, ready to fish during the long, harsh winter.*

Further afield in northern China

The culinary traditions of this region include recipes from as far north as historical Manchuria, all the way down to Henan and Shandong.

The chief characteristic of northern cooking is the frequent and lavish use of soy bean paste. This is the basis of many other pastes, such as hoisin and yellow bean, which are used to enrich sauces. Chefs in the northern regions attach great importance to the use of fresh meat and young vegetables because in the harsh terrain, with difficult transportation and no refrigeration, each region was forced to maximize the use of local products. Historically, rice was not used in northern China, but in more recent decades, due to modern transportation, northerners have discovered the versatility of this grain and adapted some of their traditional dishes to include rice.

Shandong cuisine is one of the most influential in China. The Beijing school, as well as other northern provincial styles, is thought to be a branch of Shandong style. Seafood is common, as well as wheat, millet, and other grains. Steamed breads are the choice staple.

Tianjin shares a similar cuisine with Beijing, though it uses more fish due to its coastal location. The flavours here are less heavy and rich than in Beijing.

Heilongjiang is a province criss-crossed by rivers, and its cuisine is famed for its fish dishes. Liaoning cuisine is derived from traditional native cooking styles, but it is also heavily influenced by Beijing and features strong tastes with much interplay of sweet and sour flavours. Winters here can be severe, resulting in a short growing season, and the relatively difficult climate has helped to shape the cuisine. Most dishes are rich and hearty, with wine sauces and bean pastes. The cooks here coax much from wheat, millet and soybeans, transforming them into a wide range of breads, noodles and other starchy fillers that insulate the body against the cold winter weather.

Preserving food

Jilin cuisine relies heavily on preserved foods and hearty fare owing to the harsh winters and relatively short growing seasons. Pickling is a common method of food preservation, and many households have large urns of pickled cabbage or mustard greens steeping away in their kitchens, as they do in Korea just across the border. Noodles tend to be the most common staple in Jilin cuisine.

Below *A flock of ducks is led across farmland in rural Hebei.*

Festivals and celebrations

All traditional Chinese festivals are based around the lunar calendar rather than the Gregorian calendar, and they hold a special place in the lives of Chinese people. Many Chinese celebrations have remained unchanged for centuries, with traditional dress, music and dancing still a core element. The foods that accompany the festivals are also entrenched in age-old ritual; whether in the form of special snacks, sweet cakes or savoury dishes, food plays an important role in many Chinese festivities.

The most important festival in northern China is the Spring Festival or Lunar New Year. This is a moveable feast, falling between 21 January and 19 February, depending on the phases of the new moon. It heralds the beginning of the season of fruitfulness and anticipates the harvest to come. There are many ancient and colourful rites associated with the festival, as the various regional ethnic groups celebrate it differently.

Preparing the house
During the period from the 23rd day of the previous lunar month to the festival itself, every family cleans the house from top to bottom, and stocks up on fish, meat, nuts, seeds, sweets (candies) and fruits. Every market place in northern China is ablaze with vibrant colours, from plum blossoms, oranges and tangerines to red lanterns, whole roast pigs and melon seeds dyed red for good fortune.

Chinese characters for prosperity, luck and longevity are written on red scrolls, then pasted on doors and gates, and paper pictures adorn windows. These messages originated in the Song dynasty (960–1279), and are written in a literary form characterized by concise sentences expressing wishes for the coming year.

Below Drummers perform during the Spring Festival in Beijing.

The family reunion

On the eve of the Lunar Festival, every family will try their best to assemble at the home of the eldest member, where they to enjoy the family reunion feast in which dumplings (jiaozi) are the most typical food. It is a time for old debts to be settled and differences smoothed over. It is an important Chinese belief that no one should go into the New Year bearing grudges or do anything that disrupts family harmony.

Devout Taoists burn joss sticks at ancestral altars and offer special dishes, nuts, fruits and flowers to the dead. Prayers are said to determine if the food has been received by the departed. As a mark of filial piety and respect, no one else can eat until it is agreed that the dead have received their gifts.

Festival foods and flowers

Symbolism permeates every aspect of life in Chinese culture, especially at the Lunar New Year festival. At home, families cook a special chicken soup called 'broth of prosperity', filled with egg dumplings and pigeon eggs symbolizing gold and silver ingots. The chicken represents the phoenix rising from the ashes, or rebirth and rejuvenation. Pork, duck, chicken and fish constitute the 'four heroes of the table'. Braised, seasoned pork shoulder is known as 'mist of harmony'; a combination of sea cucumber, squid and seaweed is named 'jade of ink' or 'gold of darkness'; transparent vermicelli noodles (fun si) are referred to as 'silvery threads of longevity'; platters of chicken wings are thought 'to soar one thousand miles'; and bamboo shoots are eaten because they grow so tall and inspire people to 'year after year, ascend to great heights'.

Floral tributes are another important feature of the festival. Two particularly popular flowers are narcissi, which stand for good fortune, and camellias, with their waxy blooms, which herald the coming of spring and symbolize youth and rebirth.

Lantern Festival

In the north of China, the Lunar New Year culminates in the Lantern Festival on the 15th day. Tianguan, the Taoist deity responsible for good fortune, loved all kinds of entertainment and celebrated his birthday on the 15th day of the first lunar month. In homage, fun-filled activities take place and lanterns are lit to create the ambience of gaiety that he so loved.

Above Moon cakes tend to be round, are usually made in a mould, and have Chinese symbols on top.
Above left Dumplings are steamed in the streets of Beijing to celebrate Chinese New Year.

Moon Cake Festival

This mid-autumn festival is celebrated by both the Han people and many minority nationalities in North China. Moon worship can be traced back as far as the ancient Xia and Shang dynasties (2000–1066BC). In subsequent years, Chinese people started the custom of baking 'moon cakes' stuffed with lotus seed paste as gifts for their relatives. As night falls, people come outside to gaze at the full moon, or walk by the lakes to celebrate the festival by watching the moon and its reflection.

Dragon Boat Festival

In northern China, as elsewhere in the country, this is celebrated on the 5th day of the 5th lunar month. Dumplings wrapped in lotus leaves are made and eaten, as in the rest of China; however, in the northern provinces, the dumplings are filled with both savoury meat mixtures and sweet bean paste.

Tools and equipment

Chinese cooks have traditionally used specific pans and utensils, the shape and function of which have remained almost unchanged for centuries. Natural materials of clay, metal and bamboo are still preferred to more modern electric inventions for cooking and serving food, and the most popular cooking methods rely on direct heat, such as stir-frying or steaming. This is why the simple shape of the round-based wok is such an important part of this iconic utensil – it is ideal for all kinds of cooking, and will be found in every Chinese kitchen.

Many of the utensils used in Chinese cooking are unique to that part of the world. However, Western kitchens today are likely to have at least some of the things mentioned here. If you cook Chinese food often, it is worth investing in some good equipment.

Wok

Always the most important utensil in a Chinese kitchen, the wok dates back centuries to the time of nomadic tribes in northern China. Because these people were always on the move with their animals, searching for the best grazing sites, they needed a cooking vessel with a rounded base that could sit on a few rocks over a makeshift fire. The wok was born, and its basic shape has never changed. It does multiple duty in most Chinese households, acting as a steamer, braising pan, frying pan and shallow boiler.

Electric woks are a recent innovation. They are not perfect, as the heat is moderate and does not lend itself to the high temperatures needed for rapid stir-frying. However, they work well for slow braising and steaming.

Cast iron (an alloy of iron and carbon) is still the best material for woks, though cast aluminium, being much lighter and less expensive, is increasingly used.

The traditional wok ladle is shaped at an angle that reflects the curvature of the wok. This allows for better scooping and more efficient stir-frying, as the blade has a broader area than a wooden spoon and other conventional ladles.

Frying pan

Although a wok can be used for most purposes, a frying pan is useful for frying pancakes and other things that require a flat-bottomed pan.

Cleaver

This unique Chinese knife is made of tempered iron or steel, honed to razor sharpness. The most useful size is about 30cm/12in in length and 10cm/4in wide, with a wooden handle. It provides essential leverage for cutting through bone and large pieces of meat, and is a versatile implement – it can be used as a carver, crusher, slicer and chopper.

Clay or sand pot

This Chinese dish comes with a single handle and serves as an oven-to-table utensil when food is to be served piping hot or sizzling. Traditional clay pots have a wire frame to support the structure, as

*Below left **Using a wok for deep-frying is simple and convenient.***
*Below **A frying pan is ideal for making Mandarin pancakes.***

Left *A Mongolian steamboat can be used to cook all sorts of ingredients.*

Chopsticks

For many centuries, the Chinese have used bamboo chopsticks as they have a slightly rough texture, which is best for manipulating slippery foods such as noodles and sauce-covered dishes. Normal chopsticks are 22cm/9in long, but longer ones, which can be up to twice this length, are used for turning deep-fried foods, keeping the cook at a safe distance from spitting hot oil.

Rice cookers

These are ubiquitous in Asian homes, and are no longer regarded as a novelty in the West, as many restaurants have made use of this marvellous Japanese invention. Electric models now also have features for keeping rice warm for up to an hour. These work on the principle of weight – when all the liquid has been absorbed or evaporated, the inner container, which sits on a spring-loaded element, rises automatically, switching the appliance off.

Serving dishes

Many Chinese dishes are served with a variety of accompaniments, such as dips or sauces. It is a good idea to have a few tiny dishes in which to present them.

the intense heat can cause cracks. Clay pots are never used for the whole cooking process. Dishes are cooked in a wok or other utensil and then transferred to the clay pot, which is pre-heated just enough to maintain the food's temperature at the table.

Steamboat

This unusual dish originated in Mongolia. Steamboats are sometimes called fire pots or hot pots, and are usually made of brass-coated or enamel-coated metal with a funnel in the centre of a moat. Stock or water is poured into this moat and the whole dish is heated over charcoal, although it is common today to see electric models with thermostatic controls. Various foods are cut up and placed around the steamboat so that diners can cook the food themselves, dipping pieces of food into the bubbling stock using brass wire mesh spoons.

Steamer

These are traditionally made of woven bamboo, though these days they may also be made of aluminium, with multiple perforated trays to allow the steam to rise through each layer. Steamers come in many sizes, small enough to contain bite-sized morsels (as in dim sum) or large enough to contain whole chickens. Multiple-stack steamers are ideal for cooking several dishes at the same time.

Bamboo draining baskets

Ubiquitous in all Asian countries, these versatile utensils are used for many purposes, including straining liquids, for draining soaked rice or as food covers that allow air circulation but keep out flying insects. They are the Chinese equivalent of a colander.

Right *It is handy to have a selection of small dipping bowls for serving.*

Classic ingredients

The long, cold winters that grip northern China each year have shaped the culinary landscape in a variety of ways. Firstly, the growing season is fairly short, so pickling is a popular method of preserving vegetables. Secondly, because of the harsh climate and unforgiving weather, the local people have a preference for hearty, rich and warming dishes, meaning that the local menu is packed with substantial stews. Wheat is one of the main crops, and it is transformed into starchy fillers such as noodles and steamed breads.

Beijing cuisine is typically elegant, but in an understated way. Given its imperial history, it can be surprising to find that the ingredients are often simple, with as much influence drawn from remote Mongolia as from the great dynasties of the Forbidden City.

Noodles
While rice is the fundamental staple food in southern Chinese regions where the grain grows profusely, noodles and other wheat-flour products are the favourite fillers in northern China.

*Below, left to right **Dried wheat noodles, fresh wheat noodles and fresh yellow egg noodles.***

Wheat noodles These are generally yellow in colour, ranging from pale to deep golden in hue. Today, factories all over China churn out many varieties, both dried and fresh, to be used in stir-fries or soups. Wheat noodles are sometimes enriched with egg; these tend to be sold fresh, and are firmer and denser than ordinary wheat noodles.

Dried noodles have to be boiled or blanched, but for how long depends on their type and structure; it is best to follow the packet instructions. Fresh and semi-dry noodles come with a light coating of flour and need only to be blanched. Fresh yellow egg noodles are ready for stir-frying, and need no pre-cooking or blanching.

Mung bean noodles Also known as transparent noodles, translucent vermicelli, cellophane noodles or glass noodles, these are made from mung bean flour (the same bean that yields beansprouts). They come in dried skeins that reconstitute rapidly when soaked in warm water. Mung bean noodles are very resilient, remaining firm and crunchy no matter how long you cook them. They are used in stir-fries, and are regarded as a vegetable ingredient rather than a carbohydrate staple.

Rice noodles These are not traditionally found on northern menus, as little rice is grown here. However, with modern factory production, rice noodles are now available all over China and can be incorporated into modern Mandarin cuisine.

Rice

Although it is a staple in the rest of China, rice is scarcely grown in the northern provinces. Therefore, rice rarely appears in traditional Mandarin cuisine. However, thanks to globalization and transportation, today it is enjoyed here just as it is around the rest of the world. Glutinous rice is used in some sweet snacks from Beijing.

Vegetables

Whether fresh or pickled, vegetables play a crucial role in Mandarin cuisine, appearing in every meal from the grandest to the most humble.

Bamboo shoots Technically a giant grass (known as sun jian, or simply sun, in Mandarin), bamboo enjoys a revered status in Chinese food and culture. The shoots are pale yellow or creamy white, crunchy in texture, and have a slightly astringent taste. They absorb flavourings well and keep their crunchy texture when cooked. Bamboo shoots tend to be used fresh in China, but are also available pickled or dried. They are sold in cans or jars outside of China, either as whole shoots or in slices or chunks. Soak them in cold water for 30 minutes before use.

Beansprouts These are ubiquitous throughout most of the northern provinces, with the exception of the most northerly areas. They can be eaten raw but are usually added to stir-fried noodles and cooked very briefly to give some crunch to the dish. Their flavour is delicate and watery. They are available fresh in most supermarkets, and can be stored in the refrigerator for 2–3 days.

Pak choi (Bok choy) Known as xiao bai cai in Mandarin, pak choi is usually about 13cm/5in long, with pale green stalks and dark, thin leaves. It is excellent in stir-fries and stews.

Chinese leaves (Chinese cabbage) This ingredient is sometimes known as napa cabbage, and is called bai cai in Mandarin. It has a delicate sweet aroma. The broad stalks are pale green to ivory white with a crunchy texture, and the light green leaves are slightly frilly. Chinese leaves are used in stir-fries, stews and soups, and sometimes raw in salads.

Kai lan This is a dark green vegetable that is often described as Chinese broccoli (jie lan in Mandarin) but is actually a member of the kale family. The stalks have a robust texture and taste.

Spring onions (Scallions) In China, these are regarded as a vegetable in their own right, not just a garnish. They are used in many meat and poultry dishes, and they are fundamental to dumplings.

Chinese chives These chives are found in three forms throughout China: green chives (jiu cai in Mandarin) with flat slim-bladed leaves; yellow chives (jiu huang), which are grown under a cloche or in the dark; and flowering chives (also known as garlic chives) with sturdy round stems tipped with pointed green buds. All have a pronounced onion-garlic flavour. Green chives are usually stir-fried or used to enliven dumpling and spring roll fillings, whereas yellow chives are more delicate in flavour and are ideally suited to soups.

Leeks Holding a special place in Chinese cuisine, leeks are eaten for symbolic reasons (the Mandarin name, suan, is phonetically similar to the word for 'count' – as in counting money). The white part is sliced or chopped, for an aromatic and versatile addition to many dishes.

Below, left to right **Whole and sliced bamboo shoots, beansprouts and spring onions.**

Above, left to right **Mangetouts, taro and shiitake mushrooms.**

Mangetouts (Snow peas) These flat, green peas are very crunchy and sweet, and they need minimal cooking. They can be added to vegetarian stews or chopped finely as part of a filling for spring rolls.

Aubergines (Eggplants) The most common aubergine is long and thin, in shades of pale green or purple with a faintly sweet flavour. It is an incredibly versatile vegetable – it can be steamed, fried or stuffed. The fine-textured flesh readily absorbs spices and seasonings.

Gourds and squashes The Chinese are particularly fond of cooking with gourds and squashes, which come in many shapes and sizes. They include bitter melon, luffa squash and winter melon, and are widely available in Asian markets.

Jicama This sweet turnip has a thin brown skin and tastes faintly of water chestnuts. It is known as sha ge in Mandarin.

Mooli (Daikon) This root vegetable looks like a large white carrot. It is known as lor por in Mandarin. It is crisp, juicy and slightly spicy in flavour. It can be eaten raw or cooked.

Taro This root vegetable, also known as yam (or shan yao in Mandarin), generally comes in regular and baby varieties. Baby taros are small and egg-shaped; others are about 25cm/10in long and barrel-shaped. Both are covered in short hairs, with white, purple-flecked flesh. Taro is used in much the same way as potatoes – mashed, baked or added to soups, stews and curries. The larger variety is firm with a nutty flavour; the smaller one is creamier and sweeter, lending itself to sweet dishes.

Cassava Also known as manioc or tapioca, this is a large tuber with a rough dark brown skin. Cassava (mu shu in Mandarin) is extremely versatile, mostly used in sweet dishes. It should not be eaten raw.

Ginkgo nuts Native to Henan province, as well as some western provinces, ginkgo nuts have a mild, slightly bitter taste, which makes them ideal for adding to soups and stews. They are available dried or canned in most Chinese stores.

Water chestnuts These are sold fresh in Chinese markets, with brown skins that peel away to reveal a crunchy, white nut inside. They can be eaten raw or cooked. They are sold canned in supermarkets.

Dried and preserved vegetables In the cold northern parts of China, vegetables must be preserved for the winter, when nothing fresh is available. Many types of dried vegetables are traditionally used both for their nutritional qualities and for their concentrated flavour. These include dried cole, lily buds, preserved mustard greens, preserved winter vegetable and salted vegetables.

Mushrooms

In north China, mushrooms come in all shapes, sizes, colours and textures. They are sometimes used fresh, but dried mushrooms are more common; when reconstituted, they have wonderful depth of flavour.

Shiitake Also known as Chinese black mushrooms, these have a distinctively husky flavour and are usually sold dried. They are not all black – in fact, they vary from a pale peach colour to dark greyish-brown, depending on the variety. They must be softened in warm water for about 30 minutes, after which the tough stems are removed and the caps are chopped up and added to stews, stir-fries and fillings for dim sum.

Oyster mushrooms In the wild, oyster mushrooms (pinggu in Mandarin) grow in clumps on rotting wood. The caps, gills and stems are all the same colour, which can be pearl grey, pink or yellow. Large ones should be torn, rather than cut, into pieces.

Straw mushrooms Once peeled, small dark brown caps and cream-coloured stems are revealed, which look beautiful in clear broths. The flavour and texture is very delicate. These are available in cans.

Cloud ear (Wood ear) mushrooms Thin and brittle in their dried form, cloud ears need to be soaked in water, when they swell up and resemble frilly clumps of rubbery seaweed. They expand to six or eight times their volume after soaking. When cooked, they become translucent and gelatinous, but still retain a bite. Silver ear fungus goes by the same name in Mandarin, and is used in the same way. The generic name for all types is mu er.

White fungus This type of fungus is similar to cloud ear mushrooms, but is peachy white in colour. It is called bai mu er in Mandarin, meaning 'white cloud ear'. It needs to be soaked before use, until it is soft with a jelly-like texture. White fungus is often added to soups.

Fresh fruits

The climate of northern China is generally temperate, which is ideally suited to fruit production on a grand scale. The major areas of fruit cultivation are concentrated along the Yellow River valley. Fruit tends to be eaten on its own as a snack; fruity desserts are very rare. The climate is well suited to growing apples, and they are the most important crop by far, followed by pears, peaches and grapes, and then by apricots, plums, persimmon and kiwi fruit.

Dried fruits

A variety of dried fruits are used in sweet and savoury recipes. Dates are common, with the small red dried dates being the most readily available. Longon fruits, although available fresh locally, are usually sold pitted and dried in stores outside of China.

Meat, game and offal

As in the rest of China, pork is a popular meat on the northern Chinese menu. However, due to the large Muslim population of the northern provinces, there is also plenty of lamb, mutton, goat and beef on offer.

Above, left to right **White fungus, dried red dates and pork ribs.**

Pork The way that pork is cut dictates how it is cooked in Chinese cuisine, with specific ratios of lean meat to fat to skin. The most popular local dishes are stewed spare ribs, pork and turnips, and the iconic mu shu pork, a time-honoured dish that is popular around the world.

Lamb Mutton and lamb often feature in dishes adapted to suit northern tastes, such as Tung-Po Mutton. The name is attributed to the poet Su Tung-Po, who lived in Hangzhou. Muslims from Shandong have tweaked the original pork dish to suit their religious principles, eschewing pork and alcohol, both of which featured in the original dish.

Beef Stir-fries with beef often contain bamboo shoots, especially dishes made for festivals and special occasions. Beef is usually tenderized before being stir-fried.

Game Although rare in much of China, some dishes of the northern provinces, particularly Hebei, feature game.

Offal Liver and kidneys are cooked skilfully in Mandarin cuisine. Kidneys are thought to have medicinal properties.

Above, left to right **Peking duck, quail's eggs and river trout.**

Eggs and poultry

Many rural homes have backyards where chickens and ducks are reared. Chicken is popular among Chinese cooks as it symbolizes good tidings; it is always the featured dish during the Lunar New Year celebrations and at wedding parties.
Eggs Hen's eggs, duck eggs and quail's eggs are widely available in northern China. Duck eggs are often eaten salted or as century eggs. Century eggs, also known as preserved eggs, are common in northern China. Eggs are coated in a mixture of tea, alkaline clay, salt and wood ash, then rolled in a mass of rice chaff. They are then placed in cloth-covered jars or tightly woven baskets. In about three months, the mud slowly dries and hardens into a crust, and then the eggs are ready for consumption. The yolk becomes a dark green, cream-like substance with a strong odour of sulphur and ammonia, while the white becomes a dark brown, transparent jelly with little flavour or taste. They may be difficult to find outside of China.

Chicken In China, whole chickens are rarely roasted. If a bird is to be cooked whole, it is usually braised, steamed or simmered in a stew. More often, chicken is cut into small pieces before cooking.
Duck This is a favourite food in northern China. One of the most high-profile Chinese recipes is Peking Duck, and this is now a star item on menus around the globe, not just in Beijing.

Fish and shellfish

The provinces of Liaoning, Hebei and Shandong, as well as Tianjin municipality, have coastlines along the Yellow Sea, giving them access to plenty of fresh fish. Various fish and shellfish appear in the famous Mongolian Firepot. Red-cooked fish is typical of Beijing, the colour resulting from a blend of hoisin sauce, preserved red beancurd and wine.
Sea fish Sea bass, snapper, threadfin and mullet thrive in abundance in the coastal waters off north China. Snapper has a fine texture and mild-tasting flesh, and it can be grilled, fried or steamed. The term whitefish usually refers to mullet, pomfret, porgy or other similar white-fleshed fish. Whitebait and sprats are also popular.

River fish In the tributaries of northern China, trout and carp are plentiful. Carp thrive in the small lakes and backwaters of the area, and are cooked with various aromatic mixtures. River fish tend to take pride of place on the dinner table.
Shellfish Whether they are found in rivers or oceans, prawns (shrimp) are highly prized in China. They tend to be cooked with wine, and aromatic herbs and spices. In Shandong, Sweet-and-Sour Prawns are an iconic offering, and chefs will insist that the sauce contain Kaoliang wine vinegar, a speciality of the region. Clams, scallops, and crab are also common.

Tofu and tofu products

As old as Chinese culinary history itself, tofu, or soya beancurd, is regarded as much more than a meat substitute. Rich in protein and low in calories, tofu is very bland, but absorbs other flavours well.
Fresh tofu This comes in two types – soft or firm. The soft variety, sometimes known as silken tofu, requires no more than gentle blanching or steaming. The firm variety is best in stir-fries and as fillings. Fresh tofu does not store well – it keeps for only 3–4 days in the refrigerator.

Dried tofu Also known as beancurd sticks, dried tofu is made by simmering soya bean milk until a thin skin forms on top. This skin is then lifted very carefully and hung out to dry. The sheets shrivel and take on a corrugated texture. Unlike fresh tofu, this product has a subtle and husky flavour. It needs to be soaked to soften for about 30 minutes. It features in many northern soups and stews, and is also used for sweet, herbal brews.

Fried tofu This is also known as tofu kan in Mandarin. It is made by deep-frying firm tofu until a brown skin forms. It can be used as a pocket for meat or seafood stuffing, it can be braised, or can simply be shredded and added to congee.

Pressed tofu Cubes of fresh tofu are dried and pressed until they become firm cakes with a brown skin. They are then sliced and added to stir-fries or eaten as they are. It is a favourite during Buddhist festivals, when it takes pride of place in vegetarian recipes.

Fermented tofu Fresh tofu is dried out, then marinated with salt, rice wine and spices. It is stored in brine for 6 months. It is used for marinating poultry and as a seasoning for braised dishes. It is also known as preserved beancurd or tofu ru.

Spices and flavourings

A variety of pungent and aromatic flavourings are used in Mandarin cooking, and they are always subtly balanced.

Garlic This universal bulb is used as an aromatic in many stir-fries.

Ginger Used ground, chopped or puréed, this is essential to many dishes. Pickled ginger is a popular accompaniment.

Black bean sauce Soya beans are roasted and fermented with salt, until black and pungent. They are then left whole or ground into a thick paste.

Yellow bean sauce This salty sauce is actually brown in colour, and is made from fermented soya beans.

Chilli bean paste This ingredient originates in Sichuan, but is now universally popular all over China. It is a purée of ground dried chillies and yellow bean paste.

Hoisin sauce This sweet sauce is made from yellow bean paste and sugar, and is dark mahogany in colour. It is famous for being served with Peking duck, but is also used in stews and red-cooked dishes.

Soy sauce This is an essential condiment. Light soy sauce provides seasoning to many dishes, and dark soy sauce is used as a salting agent and to add colour.

Above, left to right **Fried tofu, hoisin sauce and rice wine.**

Vinegars Black and red vinegars are essential souring agents in soups, and are also used in dips. They are usually made from rice.

Sesame oil This has a strong nutty taste and is used as a top note in soups and stir-fries. It is never used for deep-frying.

Five spice powder This mix of spices is extremely piquant, so a little goes a long way. It gives flavour to Stewed Spare Ribs.

Tea

This is China's favourite drink, and it is consumed even in the northern provinces where it does not grow. Tea leaves are used for smoking chicken and other meats, to give them a delicate perfume.

Alcoholic drinks

China has been producing alcohol from grains for thousands of years. Grain wines are produced in most provinces, with rice wine being used for cooking and drinking. More recently, beer is becoming popular, with the most famous brand coming from Qingdao (or Tsingtao) in Shandong.

Soups and dim sum

In most Chinese homes, soups and dim sum are rarely offered as appetizers; this concept is unfamiliar there. Some soups are richly studded with meat, poultry and seafood, while dim sum can be delectable bites worthy of top-class restaurants. In rural homes, soups are often regarded as complete evening sustenance, while dim sum bites take pride of place during festive seasons. Each dish is prepared with tender loving care, even when the ingredients are extremely simple.

Elegant soups and festival snacks

Today, Beijing is the political and economic hub of modern China. However, barely a decade ago, the soaring high-rises of the exuberant capital rose from a ground that was still busy with scenes from an agrarian past. Farmers pulled their ploughs across fields just a stone's throw from the urban concrete jungle, and it is this juxtaposition of old and new that underscores the essence of Mandarin cooking.

Whether simple or grand, every dish has its beginnings in the pastoral history of the region, and soups such as White Fungus Soup with Chicken or Sour-and-Hot Lamb Soup grace the farmer's table just as easily as the imperial dining room.

Some dim sum items like Prawn and Crab Wontons and Little Dragon Dumplings are now star items on menus in Chinese restaurants across the world. Each dish has been the result of a long culinary evolution that goes hand in hand with the magnificent history of the dynasties for whom Beijing was the seat of power. The fact that they are simple and inexpensive to prepare makes for their universal popularity. They do, however, require good-quality ingredients and skilful preparation, which is why they are so often associated with joyful festivals and time-honoured celebrations.

Whether steamed, shallow-fried or deep-fried, dim sum offerings tend to be served with a dip to complement the flavours of the parcel, providing the perfect balance between the sweet, salty, sour and spicy flavours.

White fungus soup with chicken

Serves 4

40g/1½oz white fungus,
  soaked until very soft and
  with a jelly-like texture
800ml/27fl oz/scant 3¼ cups
  boiling water
1 skinless chicken breast
2 garlic cloves, chopped
30ml/2 tbsp vegetable oil
30ml/2 tbsp light soy sauce
15ml/1 tbsp sesame oil
2.5ml/½ tsp ground white pepper

The rather odd-looking white fungus used here looks nothing like the rest of the mushroom family to which it belongs. Peachy white in colour, it could pass itself off as a natural sea sponge, but it is similar in texture to the more common cloud ear (wood ear) mushrooms used in Chinese cooking. It is often confused with another ingredient, which is also called 'white fungus' but which is used only in Traditional Chinese Medicine treatments. Called bai mu er (or white cloud ears in translation), the fungus used here is a characteristic ingredient of this soup from Beijing.

1 Strain the white fungus from its soaking liquid and trim off the brown woody parts. Cut the fungus into bitesize pieces.

2 Put the water into a large pan, add the chicken and cook for 15 minutes. Remove the chicken using a slotted spoon, and slice it thinly. Return the chicken slices to the stock and add the fungus. Simmer for 10 minutes.

3 Meanwhile, fry the garlic in the oil in a wok until light brown and fragrant, then add to the soup with the soy sauce, sesame oil and pepper. Adjust the seasoning to taste, and serve hot.

Cook's tip White fungus expands considerably and you will not need much. Any excess can be chilled for up to one week to be used in other stir-fries and stews.

Per portion Energy 169kcal/701kJ; Protein 9g; Carbohydrate 7g, of which sugars 0g; Fat 12g, of which saturates 2g; Cholesterol 22mg; Calcium 11mg; Fibre 1g; Sodium 452mg.

Chicken and bamboo shoot soup

Bamboo shoots, especially when cooked from raw, have a rather strong husky taste that needs to be tempered. Even when using canned shoots, you should soak them in cold water for a few minutes before use. Bamboo shoots should not overpower other ingredients, and they are best used as a flavouring and to add crunch. When you shred them finely, their aroma and taste is more subtle. They contrast well with the chicken in this soup.

1 Whisk the egg white until slightly frothy, then add the chicken strips and coat them in the egg white. Soak the bamboo shoots in cold water for 15 minutes, then rinse and drain.

2 Bring 800ml/27fl oz/scant 3¼ cups water to the boil in a large pan and add the stock cube. Turn down to a simmer. Meanwhile, heat the fat in a wok and fry the ginger for 1 minute, then add the chicken. Stir-fry for 1 minute, then transfer the chicken and ginger to the hot stock.

3 Add the bamboo shoots and simmer for 10 minutes. Add the soy sauce and pepper, then simmer for 5 minutes.

4 Blend the cornflour with 15ml/2 tbsp water and add to soup. Stir until it thickens a little, then serve immediately.

Variation Pork strips also work well with this soup, but use a cut that has some streaky fat for a better flavour.

Serves 4

1 egg white
1 skinless chicken breast,
  sliced into thin strips
115g/4oz bamboo shoots,
  sliced into fine julienne strips
1 chicken stock (bouillon) cube
15ml/1 tbsp lard or white cooking
  fat, or vegetable oil
5ml/1 tsp grated fresh root ginger
15ml/1 tbsp light soy sauce
2.5ml/½ tsp ground black pepper
15ml/1 tbsp cornflour (cornstarch)

Per portion Energy 94kcal/393kJ; Protein 9g;
Carbohydrate 4g, of which sugars 0g; Fat 4g,
of which saturates 1g; Cholesterol 22mg;
Calcium 9mg; Fibre 1g; Sodium 537mg.

Chicken, pea and tomato soup

There are an estimated 3.5 million Muslims scattered all over China, and their diet, while fundamentally Chinese, does not include any pork. This soup, also known as Three Pearls Soup, is a typical Muslim offering from Shandong province, using tiny chicken nuggets, peas and chopped tomatoes. It is a hearty soup flavoured with wine, and is usually served during the cold winter months – Shandong winters can plunge to a shivering -15°C/5°F! This is a very pretty dish to serve to guests – when the soup is cooked, it looks as if it is awash with little coloured pearls.

1 Mince (grind) the chicken and mix it with the salt and cornflour. Whisk the egg white until slightly frothy, then add the ground chicken mixture and combine well.

2 Plunge the tomatoes into boiling water for 30 seconds, then refresh in cold water. Peel away the skins, remove the seeds and chop the flesh into small dice.

3 Bring 800ml/27fl oz/scant 3¼ cups water to the boil in a large pan, then add the sesame oil, stock cube, soy sauce and wine or sherry.

4 When it is bubbling, use two teaspoons to drop in nuggets of chicken mixture so that they form small chicken balls. Once all the chicken mixture has been added, cook for 5 minutes.

5 Add the tomatoes and peas, and simmer for 5 minutes more. Serve hot.

Serves 4

1 skinless chicken breast
2.5ml/½ tsp salt
5ml/1 tsp cornflour (cornstarch)
1 egg white
2 large tomatoes
30ml/2 tbsp sesame oil
1 chicken stock (bouillon) cube
30ml/2 tbsp light soy sauce
45ml/3 tbsp Shaoxing wine
  or dry sherry
75g/3oz/¾ cup green peas

Cook's tip Tomatoes can be substituted with something of a similar colour, such as diced ham or sliced red radishes.

Per portion Energy 187kcal/799kJ; Protein 12g; Carbohydrate 8g, of which sugars 5g; Fat 11g, of which saturates 2g; Cholesterol 33mg; Calcium 22mg; Fibre 2g; Sodium 1016mg.

Chicken and prawn ball soup

Chinese cuisine is particularly known for combining the most unlikely ingredients, like the chicken and seafood used here – and the result is fabulous. This unusual soup hails from Henan and blends the two distinctly different flavours exceptionally well. In many cases, prawns are used primarily to enhance the flavour of soups, as here, aided by sesame oil, wine and soy sauce, which work together wonderfully.

1 Heat the oil in a wok and fry the garlic for 2 minutes, then drain, reserving the oil, and set aside.

2 Bring 800ml/27fl oz/scant 3¼ cups water to the boil in a large pan and add the reserved garlic-flavoured oil and the stock cube. Add the chicken and simmer for 15 minutes.

3 Meanwhile, mince (grind) the prawns and mix with the cornflour, sesame oil and salt. Shape the mixture into small balls and drop into the soup. Cook for 5 minutes more.

4 Add the soy sauce and wine or sherry, then simmer for a further 5 minutes, until the chicken and prawn balls are cooked through.

5 Adjust the seasoning to taste, then serve hot, garnished with spring onions.

Cook's tip Adding cornflour (cornstarch) to any minced (ground) meat or seafood gives it a very smooth texture, and is much used in Chinese cuisine.

Serves 4

30ml/2 tbsp vegetable oil
2 garlic cloves, crushed
1 chicken stock (bouillon) cube
1 skinless chicken breast,
  cut into 1cm/½in dice
250g/9oz raw prawns
  (shrimp), shelled
5ml/1 tsp cornflour (cornstarch)
15ml/1 tbsp sesame oil
2.5ml/½ tsp salt
15ml/1 tbsp light soy sauce
30ml/2 tbsp Shaoxing wine
  or dry sherry
chopped spring onions (scallions),
  to garnish

Per portion Energy 169kcal/706kJ; Protein 19g; Carbohydrate 2g, of which sugars 0g; Fat 8g, of which saturates 1g; Cholesterol 144mg; Calcium 55mg; Fibre 0g; Sodium 884mg.

Tofu and minced pork soup

This is classic blend of ingredients makes a style of soup that is popular not only regionally but also nationally. In Henan, Hunan and Sichuan, this soup is cooked with various seasonings, and some will be thickened with cornflour whereas others are enriched with wine. The Sichuan version is usually fiery with chopped chillies. It is a dish that allows a chef to use his ingenuity.

1 Mix the minced pork with the cornflour and pepper. Bring 800ml/27fl oz/scant 3¼ cups water to the boil in a large pan and add the soy sauce and sesame oil. Add the bean curd and pork, stirring vigorously with a pair of chopsticks to separate the pork so that it does not form uneven lumps. Simmer for 5 minutes.

2 When the pork is properly distributed, beat the eggs lightly and add to the soup, stirring. Cook for 5 minutes, or until the soup is thick and the egg is well incorporated. You might get streaks of egg here and there, but this is perfectly normal. Garnish with spring onion and winter vegetable, and serve in individual bowls.

Variation If you like, you can garnish with fried garlic or shallots to give the soup a crispy and aromatic edge.

Serves 4

250g/9oz/generous 1 cup minced (ground) pork
5ml/1 tsp cornflour (cornstarch)
2.5ml/½ tsp ground black pepper
30ml/2 tbsp light soy sauce
30ml/2 tbsp sesame oil
250g/9oz firm tofu, cut into 1cm/½in cubes
2 eggs
1 spring onion (scallion), finely sliced on the diagonal, and 5ml/1 tsp preserved winter vegetable (tung cai or tong choy), to garnish

Per portion Energy 244kcal/1014kJ; Protein 23g; Carbohydrate 2g, of which sugars 0g; Fat 16g, of which saturates 3g; Cholesterol 155mg; Calcium 345mg; Fibre 1g; Sodium 448mg.

Serves 4

1 meat stock (bouillon) cube

200g/7oz lamb fillet, cut into
  1cm/½in cubes

200g/7oz white radish or mooli
  (daikon), peeled and cut into
  1cm/½in cubes

30ml/2 tbsp black or red rice vinegar

5ml/1 tsp Sichuan peppercorns,
  finely ground

30ml/2 tbsp dark soy sauce

2.5ml/½ tsp salt

15ml/1 tbsp cornflour (cornstarch)

crispy fried onions, to garnish

Variation For a less intense sourness,
use malt or balsamic vinegar instead
of Chinese red or black vinegar.

Per portion Energy 128kcal/534kJ; Protein 11g;
Carbohydrate 5g, of which sugars 1g; Fat 7g,
of which saturates 3g; Cholesterol 38mg;
Calcium 20mg; Fibre 1g; Sodium 904mg.

Sour-and-hot lamb soup

As hearty soups go, this Henan staple echoes that of Sichuan with its blend of hot and sour flavours. Lamb is the preferred meat in the north, but this soup is usually made with local goat, termed 'mutton', which can be a tough meat. In the West, 'mutton' refers to the meat of older sheep. Ordinary lamb will do as well and it also takes less time to cook.

1 Bring 1 litre/1¾ pints/4 cups water and the stock cube to the boil in a large pan. Add the lamb and cook, uncovered, for 25 minutes over a high heat. The stock will have reduced to about 800ml/27fl oz/scant 3¼ cups and the lamb will be almost tender. Reduce the heat and simmer until tender to your liking.

2 Add the radish to the pan and simmer for 10 minutes, then add the vinegar, Sichuan peppercorns, soy sauce and salt to taste.

3 Just before serving, blend the cornflour with a little water and add to soup. Stir until thickened, then serve.

Prawn and crab wontons

Wontons are a Cantonese invention but, over time, they have become ubiquitous throughout China, containing different fillings. These dumplings are very easy to make and lend themselves to deep-frying, steaming or adding to soups. It is important to work quickly when using wonton skins – after making the wontons, do not let them stand for too long before cooking, as the skins can become brittle when exposed to the air.

1 Wash the prawns and then mince (grind) them very finely. Mix with the crab meat and mashed tofu, then add the beaten egg and mix until well combined.

2 Add the soy sauce, sesame oil, black pepper and cornflour. Stir again and divide into 16 equal portions.

3 Put one portion of the mixture on to a wonton skin and fold up into a half-moon shape, sealing the edge with a little water. (If the skins are square, fold them into triangles.) Repeat with the other wonton skins.

4 Either deep-fry the wontons until golden brown, or steam them for 10 minutes. Serve with a chilli sauce dip.

Variation Tofu is added here, but you can also use the same amount of minced (ground) pork instead, if you prefer.

Cook's tip Wonton skins are made from flour and are available in all Chinese stores, either as 7.5cm/3in squares or circles of the same diameter.

Serves 4

250g/9oz prawns (shrimp), shelled
250g/9oz white crab meat
115g/4oz tofu, finely mashed
1 egg, lightly beaten
30ml/2 tbsp light soy sauce
15ml/1 tbsp sesame oil
2.5ml/½ tsp ground black pepper
5ml/1 tsp cornflour (cornstarch)
16 wonton skins
vegetable oil, for deep-frying (optional)
chilli sauce, to serve

Per portion Energy 451kcal/874kJ; Protein 30g; Carbohydrate 13g, of which sugars 1g; Fat 31g, of which saturates 4g; Cholesterol 225mg; Calcium 207mg; Fibre 1g; Sodium 762mg.

Sesame-coated chicken

The use of aromatic little sesame seeds is common all over China. They appear in dim sum, sprinkled on stir-fries, ground into a cream or, as here, are used to coat pieces of meat or chicken for deep-frying. They have a delicate, nutty fragrance. When processed into sesame oil, they are indispensable in a host of Chinese dishes across the regions. Sesame seeds are either pale beige or jet black in colour. They brown very quickly, so watch your oil temperature when frying these delicious morsels.

1 To make the dip, mix the garlic with the black or rice vinegar in a small serving bowl, and add the salt. Set aside.

2 Slice through each chicken breast horizontally to make eight thin escalopes in total (four from each breast). Place between sheets of clear film (plastic wrap) and tenderize lightly by beating with a rolling pin. Season with sesame oil and soy sauce.

3 Place the egg in a shallow dish and the sesame seeds on to a plate. Coat each slice of chicken liberally with egg, then make a tight roll and roll it in the sesame seeds to coat evenly. Pat the seeds to help them stay firmly in place.

4 Deep-fry the chicken rolls in the vegetable oil over a medium heat until golden brown, and serve with the vinegar and garlic dip.

Variation You can also use minced (ground) chicken or pork. Shape into small balls and coat in sesame seeds before frying.

Serves 4

2 skinless chicken breasts
15ml/1 tbsp sesame oil
15ml/1 tbsp light soy sauce
1 egg, beaten
25g/1oz/¼ cup sesame seeds
vegetable oil, for deep-frying

For the vinegar and garlic dip
4 garlic cloves, crushed
60ml/4 tbsp of black or rice vinegar
a pinch of salt

Per portion Energy 168kcal/701kJ; Protein 19g; Carbohydrate 1g, of which sugars 0g; Fat 10g, of which saturates 2g; Cholesterol 102mg; Calcium 56mg; Fibre 1g; Sodium 259mg.

 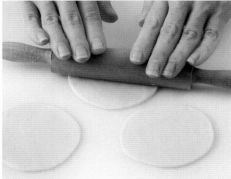 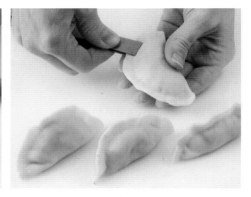

Little dragon dumplings

Within the dim sum menu, these dumplings, called xiao long bau in Mandarin, are among the most popular. How their name came about remains a mystery, but the dragon reigns supreme in Chinese culture as the most noble of heraldic beasts. Traditionally, these dumplings encase a little soup, the inclusion of which requires years of training. Imagine biting into a soft, steamed dumpling that contains a tablespoon or two of hot soup! I'm afraid this is beyond all but the most expert chefs, and even dim sum houses rarely add the soup. High-gluten flour is necessary for making the dough; it is available in most Chinese stores.

1 To make the filling, first roughly mince (grind) the prawns, then combine them with the minced pork and cornflour.

2 Add 60ml/4 tbsp water, the Chinese celery, spring onions, soy sauce, sesame oil, pepper and sugar. Stir well until flavours are incorporated, and set aside.

3 Mix the flours in a bowl and pour over the boiling water. Add the oil or fat, and stir with a wooden spoon. As soon as the mixture is cool enough to handle, knead it on a floured work surface for 5 minutes. You may find the dough rather crumbly, but, as you work, keep scooping up the floury parts and kneading them into the dough.

4 Continue to knead until the dough is smooth and elastic (like bread dough). Roll out into a long sausage shape, 2cm/¾in in diameter. Cut it into 12 pieces and shape into small balls.

5 With a rolling pin, flatten each piece until paper-thin. The dough is very elastic, and will not break. Put a tablespoonful of filling on to each 'skin' and wrap it into a half-moon shape.

6 Seal and crimp the edges; shape each dumpling so that the crimped edge is lying across the top of the dumpling, rather like a Cornish pasty. Place the dumplings on a lightly oiled plate that will fit into your steamer and steam for 15 minutes, or until the skins become slightly translucent. Serve warm with a soy or chilli sauce dip.

Makes 12 dumplings

200g/7oz high gluten flour (gou garn fun), plus extra for dusting
75g/3oz/⅔ cup plain (all-purpose) flour
200ml/7fl oz/scant 1 cup boiling water
30ml/2 tbsp vegetable oil, lard or white cooking fat
soy sauce or chilli sauce, to serve

For the filling
200g/7oz raw prawns (shrimp), shelled
200g/7oz/1¾ cups minced (ground) pork
5ml/1 tsp cornflour (cornstarch)
15ml/1 tbsp chopped Chinese celery
3 spring onions (scallions), chopped
30ml/2 tbsp light soy sauce
30ml/2 tbsp sesame oil
2.5ml/½ tsp ground black pepper
a pinch of sugar

Cook's tip This is a basic dough that can be used for a whole range of dim sum dumplings. The consistency of the cooked dough depends on how thinly you roll it out.

Per portion Energy 482kcal/2027kJ; Protein 28g; Carbohydrate 55g, of which sugars 1g; Fat18g, of which saturates 3g; Cholesterol 129mg; Calcium 145mg; Fibre 3g; Sodium 493mg.

Lotus leaf dumplings

Rice, fish, shellfish, meat and all manner of other ingredients are cooked, wrapped in lotus leaves and steamed in provinces all over China. Cantonese dim sum menus invariably feature lotus leaf-wrapped glutinous rice; other regional cuisines use lotus leaves to wrap sweet desserts and, in Beijing, they encase delectable savoury dumplings. The leaves are very large but can be trimmed to make more dainty parcels, each one a delicious combination of pork, lotus seeds and succulent quail's eggs.

1 Heat the oil in a wok and fry the garlic for 2 minutes. Add the pork and stir-fry for 3 minutes, or until sealed all over.

2 Add the mushrooms and lotus seeds, then fry for 2 minutes.

3 Add the quail's eggs, celery, oyster sauce, wine or dry sherry, pepper and soy sauce, then stir gently so that you do not to break up the delicate quail's eggs.

4 Blend the cornflour with 75ml/5 tbsp water and add to the pan. Stir until the cornflour thickens the sauce and binds all the ingredients together. Transfer the filling to a bowl and set aside.

5 Trim the lotus leaves and cut each into two fan-shaped halves. Divide the mixture between the four leaf halves (there should be about 45ml/3 tbsp on each), making sure there is a good mixture of pork, mushrooms, lotus seeds and quail's eggs in each parcel. Wrap each parcel securely, folding over the sides. Steam for 15 minutes, then serve immediately – the parcels should be opened at the table.

Cook's tips

• Quail's eggs take about 3 minutes to hard-boil.
• If the lotus leaves appear to be brittle, use a double layer for extra strength. They are actually quite resilient and do not tear easily.

Serves 4

30ml/2 tbsp vegetable oil
2 garlic cloves, crushed
200g/7oz belly pork, diced
8 Chinese mushrooms, soaked and chopped
16 canned lotus seeds
16 quail's eggs, hard-boiled and peeled
20g/³⁄₄oz chopped Chinese celery leaves
30ml/2 tbsp oyster sauce
30ml/2 tbsp Shaoxing wine or dry sherry
5ml/1 tsp ground black pepper
15ml/1 tbsp dark soy sauce
10ml/2 tsp cornflour (cornstarch)
2 lotus leaves, soaked until soft

Per portion Energy 309kcal/1289kJ; Protein 16g; Carbohydrate 10g, of which sugars 0g; Fat 22g, of which saturates 6g; Cholesterol 192mg; Calcium 39mg; Fibre 1g; Sodium 590mg.

Beef and mushroom dumplings

This is a typical steamed dim sum dish from Henan, which is sometimes made with minced lamb. Here, however, minced beef is used. Seasonings for dumplings in northern China tend to be on the heavy, heady side with the addition of wine to give a rich flavour.

1 To make the dip, peel and grate the ginger, and chop the spring onion very finely. Place them in a bowl with the black vinegar and salt. Mix well, then set aside.

2 To make the filling, mix the minced beef with the cornflour, oyster sauce, wine or sherry, pepper, spring onion and ginger. Chop the mushrooms finely and add to the beef mixture. Mix together well and set aside.

3 Mix the flours in a mixing bowl, and pour over the boiling water. Add the oil or fat, and stir with a wooden spoon. As soon as the mixture is cool enough to handle, transfer it to a floured work surface and knead for 5 minutes. You may find the dough rather crumbly, but, as you work, keep scooping up the floury parts and kneading them into the dough.

4 Continue to knead until the dough is smooth and elastic (it should have the consistency of bread dough). Roll out into a long sausage shape, 2cm/³⁄₄in in diameter. Cut it into 12 pieces and shape into small balls.

5 With a rolling pin, flatten each piece until it is paper-thin. It will not break, as the dough is very elastic. Put a tablespoonful of filling on to each 'skin' and fold it over into a half-moon shape.

6 Seal and crimp the edges; shape each dumpling so that the crimped edge is lying across the top of the dumpling, rather like a Cornish pasty. Place the dumplings on a lightly oiled plate that will fit into your steamer and steam for 15 minutes, or until the skins become slightly translucent. Serve warm with the dip.

Cook's tip This dough can be kept chilled and covered for a day or two, if you have any left over. It can be filled with a range of vegetarian or meat fillings.

Makes 12 dumplings

200g/7oz high gluten flour (gou garn
  fun), plus extra for dusting
75g/3oz/²⁄₃ cup plain (all-purpose) flour
200ml/7fl oz/scant 1 cup boiling water
30ml/2 tbsp vegetable oil,
  lard or white cooking fat

For the dip
25g/1oz fresh root ginger
1 spring onion (scallion)
75ml/5 tbsp black vinegar
a pinch of salt

For the filling
400g/14oz/3¹⁄₂ cups minced
  (ground) beef
5ml/1 tsp cornflour (cornstarch)
30ml/2 tbsp oyster sauce
15ml/1 tbsp Shaoxing wine
  or dry sherry
2.5ml/¹⁄₂ tsp ground black pepper
1 spring onion (scallion),
  finely chopped
15ml/1 tbsp ground ginger
8 Chinese mushrooms,
  soaked until soft

Per portion Energy 177kcal/766kJ; Protein 10g;
Carbohydrate 21g, of which sugars 1g; Fat 6g,
of which saturates 2g; Cholesterol 19mg;
Calcium 42mg; Fibre 1g; Sodium 153mg.

Beef cakes

Usually served at festive occasions, these are a meaty variation of onion pancakes, which are more common on world-wide dim sum menus. Beef cakes make hearty snacks and can be made well in advance, then warmed up or lightly re-fried. They go very well with the vinegar, ginger and spring onion dip on page 42. The traditional recipe uses solid pork fat, chopped and added to the beef for crunch and succulence. This may be hard to find, so use bacon rind as a substitute – it gives a nice, smoky flavour.

1 Place all the filling ingredients in a bowl and mix together thoroughly. Pinch off a small ball, cook it quickly in a small pan, then taste to check the seasoning. Adjust the seasoning, if necessary. Cook the rest of the mixture in the pan for about 5 minutes until the beef is cooked through, then set it aside to cool.

2 Sift the flours into a mixing bowl and add the salt. Mix well and gradually add the boiling water, stirring well. Add the 15ml/1 tbsp vegetable oil. When cool enough to handle, transfer the dough to a floured surface, and knead for 5 minutes, until smooth.

3 Roll out into a long sausage shape and cut into eight pieces. Flatten each piece into a thin circle about 9cm/3½in in diameter, or as thin as you can make them without breaking them. Divide the beef mixture between the eight circles (there should be a heaped tablespoonful on each). Draw the sides in to the centre, then pinch to seal firmly. Smooth the sealed sides, then shape and flatten them gently into round, flat cakes with the sealed side underneath.

4 Heat a frying pan with the 75ml/5 tbsp oil and fry the cakes, in batches, for 3 minutes on each side, or until golden brown. Add more oil, if necessary, for each batch, but heat it up before adding the remaining cakes.

Variation As a vegetarian option, substitute the minced (ground) beef and pork fat with the equivalent weight of chopped leeks and mushrooms.

Makes 8

200g/7oz/1¾ cups plain (all-purpose) flour, plus extra for dusting
40g/1½oz/⅓ cup tapioca flour
a pinch of salt
200ml/7fl oz/scant 1 cup boiling water
15ml/1 tbsp vegetable oil, plus about 75ml/5 tbsp for frying

For the filling
200g/7oz/1¾ cups minced (ground) beef
75g/3oz pork fat or bacon fat, finely chopped
45ml/3 tbsp water
30ml/2 tbsp light soy sauce
2.5ml/½ tsp ground black pepper
2 spring onions (scallions), finely chopped
25g/1oz fresh root ginger, grated
a pinch of sugar
30ml/2 tbsp sesame oil

Per portion Energy 304kcal/1268kJ; Protein 10g; Carbohydrate 25g, of which sugars 1g; Fat 19g, of which saturates 4g; Cholesterol 20mg; Calcium 44mg; Fibre 1g; Sodium 232mg.

Fish and shellfish

Northern China may not be blessed with the endless coastal strips of eastern and southern China, but the coastlines of Shandong, Tianjin, Hebei and Liaoning offer good hauls. The delta and numerous tributaries of the Yellow River also offer surprising bounty. The Chinese recognize the important culinary difference between sea and river fish, and this is reflected in their recipes. Even in the farthest reaches of ancient Manchuria, fish and shellfish dishes come into their own, showing how inland regions have long put their local river catches to use.

Delicate river and ocean catches

I am lucky enough to have spent much time in Beijing, and had the pleasure of dining in some of the city's most famous restaurants, as well as sampling various dishes from its street food menus; I came away as sated with one as the other.

Beijing cuisine has been influenced greatly by that of Shandong throughout history, so good quality fish and shellfish dishes take pride of place on many a restaurant menu. Prawns (shrimp) and scallops are cooked to perfection, and both sea and river fish are given special treatment by top chefs.

At the other end of the spectrum is the wonderful street food; the glorious sights, smells and sounds showcasing the vendor's deft wok skills as he stirs up fiery concoctions of succulent fish and shellfish. From Sweet-and-Sour Prawns to scrumptious Mock Crab Cakes, the fish and shellfish plates from this region are exemplary. Carp, trout, snapper and grouper get the most refined treatment, regardless of the street or restaurant backdrop.

With chefs becoming more travel-wise, and learning from each other, there is now a stronger influence from other regions being displayed in Mandarin food. A perfect example is the Mongolian Seafood Steamboat, which is now cooked in restaurants across the country. Its beginnings, in the remote northern areas, may have been traditionally rustic, but as a dining experience it has become the epitome of creative Chinese cooking. It makes a truly memorable meal.

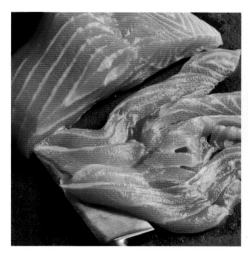

Raw fish salad

In the past, I must admit that the provinces in the extreme north-east did not hold much fascination for me. This is possibly because so little is known about Liaoning, Heilongjiang and Jilin. Several years ago, two doctors from Liaoning moved in next door to me, and from them I learned about this far-flung region and sampled the wonderful food. Liaoning cuisine is heavily influenced by Beijing and features strong tastes, with interplay between sweet-and-sour flavours. This Liaoning raw fish salad is integral to Lunar New Year repasts, as its name, yu sheng, means 'rebirth' in Mandarin.

1 Freeze the salmon for 20 minutes so that it firms up – this will make slicing it much easier. Using a sharp knife, slice the fillet thinly across the grain, then chill the fish slices while you prepare the vegetables.

2 Slice the pickled ginger, green carrot, iceberg lettuce, radish or mooli and spring onions into extremely fine pieces and soak them in cold water for 15 minutes.

3 Drain the vegetables thoroughly and transfer them to a serving bowl. Add the sliced salmon, and toss everything together.

4 Mix all the dressing ingredients together in a small bowl, taste and adjust the seasonings as necessary. Pour the dressing over the fish and vegetables, and toss to coat everything. Serve, garnished with fried garlic or shallots.

Cook's tips
• Green carrots are not unripe carrots but a specific genus. They are a seasonal ingredient and therefore not always available. Use normal carrots instead, if you cannot find them.
• For any raw fish dish it is essential to buy the freshest fish possible. Always check with your fishmonger first that it is suitable for eating raw.

Serves 4

450g/1lb salmon fillet, skin removed
  (wild salmon is best)
20g/³⁄₄oz pickled ginger
75g/3oz green carrot
  (*see* Cook's Tip)
75g/3oz iceberg lettuce
75g/3oz white radish or
  mooli (daikon)
2 spring onions (scallions)
fried garlic or shallots, to garnish

For the dressing
a pinch of ground cinnamon
2.5ml/¹⁄₂ tsp Chinese
  five-spice powder
45ml/3 tbsp rice vinegar
2.5ml/¹⁄₂ tsp sugar
2.5ml/¹⁄₂ tsp salt
15ml/1 tbsp sesame oil
30ml/2 tbsp plum sauce

Per portion Energy 263kcal/1093kJ; Protein 23g; Carbohydrate 5g, of which sugars 5g; Fat 16g, of which saturates 3g; Cholesterol 56mg; Calcium 47mg; Fibre 1g; Sodium 309mg.

Sweet-and-sour prawns

Shandong is believed to be the birthplace of sweet-and-sour dishes but, being such an enticing blend, the technique has crossed many borders, and is a particular favourite in Shanxi. It has also leapt oceans and is now an iconic national Chinese delicacy in just about every corner of the earth. Northern chefs will insist that the sauce should contain kaoliang wine vinegar made from sorghum and millet grains. If this is unavailable, use any ordinary Chinese rice wine vinegar. Whichever primary ingredient you use – be it seafood, meat or poultry – it is the sauce that makes the dish.

1 Make a shallow cut down the centre of the curved back of each prawn. Pull out the black vein with a cocktail stick (toothpick) or your fingers, then rinse the prawns thoroughly.

2 Dust the prawns with cornflour, then shake off the excess. Heat the oil in a wok and shallow fry the prawns briefly until they are just cooked but with a slightly crispy coating. Remove with a slotted spoon, and set aside.

3 In the oil remaining in the wok, fry the garlic for 2 minutes, then add the onion. Fry for 2 minutes, then add the water chestnuts and red pepper. Fry for 1 minute.

4 Blend the sauce ingredients together in a measuring cup, then add to the pan. Bring to the boil and cook for 1 minute.

5 Add the prawns and stir well to incorporate. Cook for 2 minutes and serve hot.

Serves 4

450g/1lb king prawns (jumbo shrimp), shelled, but with tails left on
30ml/2 tbsp cornflour (cornstarch)
45ml/3 tbsp vegetable oil
15ml/1 tbsp crushed garlic
1 onion, quartered
12 water chestnuts, drained and sliced in half
½ red (bell) pepper, thinly sliced

For the sauce
60ml/4 tbsp kaoliang wine vinegar or rice wine vinegar
45ml/3 tbsp plum sauce
2.5ml/½ tsp sugar
200ml/7fl oz/scant 1 cup water or stock

Cook's tip If you are short of time, omit the first frying step for the prawns. Instead, add them at step 3, then cook until they turn completely pink. There is no difference in taste and only a marginal one in texture.

Per portion Energy 266kcal/1114kJ; Protein 21g; Carbohydrate 15g, of which sugars 6g; Fat 12g, of which saturates 1g; Cholesterol 219mg; Calcium 99mg; Fibre 2g; Sodium 308mg.

Prawn cutlets

In the inland areas of northern China, you can see fishermen in small boats throwing large nets into the rivers and dragging them to catch prawns, as well as squid and fish. The catches are often sold immediately on the riverbanks. Prawns this fresh have an extra-special flavour when they are cooked. Most of us are not able to buy prawns direct from the fishing boat, but do try to buy the freshest ones you can.

1 Place all the dips and accompaniments into individual bowls and set aside.

2 Mince (grind) the prawns until fine. Mash the tofu with a fork until smooth, then mix with the prawns. Add the sesame oil, soy sauce and pepper, and blend well.

3 Beat the eggs lightly and add to the mixture. Stir well to combine. Shape into four patties, each about 6cm/2½in in diameter and 1cm/½in thick.

4 Heat the oil for deep-frying in a wok or deep-fryer. Coat the patties with cornflour and deep-fry them until golden brown and cooked through. Serve immediately, with the dips and accompaniments.

Variation The same weight of mashed potato can be used as a binding agent instead of tofu.

Serves 4

450g/1lb prawns (shrimp), shelled
200g/7oz firm tofu
15ml/1 tbsp sesame oil
15ml/1 tbsp light soy sauce
5ml/1 tsp ground black pepper
2 eggs
45ml/3 tbsp cornflour (cornstarch)
vegetable oil, for deep-frying

For the accompaniments
English (hot) or Dijon mustard
chilli sauce
black vinegar
1 cucumber, sliced into thin rounds
75g/3oz pickled ginger

Per portion Energy 332kcal/1386kJ; Protein 28g; Carbohydrate 11g, of which sugars 0g; Fat 20g, of which saturates 3g; Cholesterol 335mg; Calcium 365mg; Fibre 0g; Sodium 443mg.

Fresh scallops and pak choi

Here is a dish with a true imperial flavour, one that Shandong citizens are extremely proud of as a banqueting dish. Use the best scallops you can find – each one large and about 1cm/½in thick. The pak choi here is of the smaller variety, sometimes called Taiwan pak choi, with pale green stalks and dark green leaves. This is sometimes served with the pak choi arranged to look like the spokes of a wheel, with the scallops on top.

1 Trim off the hard root end of the pak choi, while leaving them whole and as complete stalks. Bring a pan of water to the boil and blanch the pak choi for 1 minute, then drain. Blanch the scallops for 20 seconds, then drain.

2 Heat the oil in a wok and fry the ginger and garlic for 2 minutes. Add the sesame oil, wine or sherry, salt, pepper and sugar. Stir for 30 seconds, then add the pak choi and scallops.

3 Continue to stir-fry for 1 minute, then serve immediately.

Variation Vegetables such as mangetouts (snow peas), courgettes (zucchini) and green beans also make a good contrast. Blanch them in place of the pak choi.

Serves 4

300g/11oz pak choi (bok choy)
300g/11oz fresh scallops
15ml/1 tbsp vegetable oil
15ml/1 tbsp ground ginger
15ml/1 tbsp crushed garlic
15ml/1 tbsp sesame oil
30ml/2 tbsp Shaoxing wine
  or dry sherry
2.5ml/½ tsp salt
2.5ml/½ tsp ground black pepper
a pinch of sugar
15ml/1 tbsp cornflour (cornstarch)

Per portion Energy 162kcal/674kJ; Protein 13g; Carbohydrate 7g, of which sugars 1g; Fat 8g, of which saturates 1g; Cholesterol 24mg; Calcium 57mg; Fibre 1g; Sodium 344mg.

Serves 4

350g/12oz meaty white fish, such as
  cod or halibut
115g/4oz tofu, mashed
1 egg, lightly beaten
15ml/1 tbsp cornflour (cornstarch)
15ml/1 tbsp rice flour
2 spring onions (scallions),
  finely chopped
3 garlic cloves, crushed
15ml/1 tbsp sesame oil
15ml/1 tbsp light soy sauce
2.5ml/½ tsp ground black pepper
vegetable oil, for deep-frying
thinly sliced cucumber and a chilli
  sauce dip, to serve

Variation For a vegetarian
alternative, use a mixture of minced
(ground) vegetables, such as
mushrooms, marrow (large zucchini)
and carrots, for the mock crab.

Per portion Energy 270kcal/1123kJ; Protein 21g;
Carbohydrate 18g, of which sugars 1g; Fat 17g,
of which saturates 2g; Cholesterol 98mg;
Calcium 178mg; Fibre 0g; Sodium 257mg.

Mock crab cakes

The Chinese believe that a 'mock' anything is better than none at all, and this philosophy gave birth to a school of cooking using gluten to represent meat, chicken and poultry, one loved by Buddhist vegetarians. You may well ask why they would want meat-free dishes to look like meat? This question has been debated by food historians for centuries. These patties were concocted for the Empress Dowager of the Qing Dynasty who, being fond of crab that was unfortunately then out of season, was served a fishy version. Her Imperial Majesty loved it, and no heads rolled.

1 Steam the fish for 10 minutes, then cool, flake and mash until fine. Thoroughly mix the tofu and egg with the fish, cornflour and rice flour.

2 Add the spring onions, garlic, sesame oil, soy sauce and pepper. Stir well and shape into small patties about 4cm/1½in in diameter and 1cm/½in thick. Deep-fry until golden brown, and serve with sliced cucumber and a chilli sauce dip.

Mongolian seafood steamboat

Probably one of the oldest forms of social entertainment, a Mongolian steamboat is a really festive winter warmer, a convivial repast meant for at least six people, all seated around the bubbling centrepiece. Steamboats are also called hot-pots and date back to early Mongolian times. The technique also appears in Japan and Korea, both countries having their own styles, known as shabu shabu and sinsulo respectively. The traditional utensil is a large brass pan with a built-in funnel in the centre; charcoal is put in the space directly under the funnel and lit. Stock is then poured into the moat and, when it boils, diners immerse the foods of their choice to cook in the stock using wire mesh spoons. Today, steamboats may be charcoal or electric with a thermostatic control.

1 Preheat the steamboat and fill the moat with boiling water. Add the stock cubes. Have a kettle standing by with more water for topping up as the meal goes on.

2 While the stock is simmering, arrange all the seasonings and the main ingredients in plates and bowls set around the steamboat. Provide a wire mesh spoon, a porcelain soup spoon, chopsticks and a soup bowl for each person. (These are all available in Chinese stores.)

3 To cook and eat, each person puts a few pieces of selected raw foods into their wire mesh spoon and dunks it into the boiling stock until cooked, then they transfer it to their individual soup bowl and add seasonings, dips and garnishes to their liking.

4 When all the ingredients are eaten, the stock will be extremely rich. It can then be ladled into each bowl to drink with a spoon.

Cook's tips

• Stock cubes are handy, but for better flavour, make your own stock.
• The selection of ingredients is entirely personal and there is no set formula. Meat, seafood, poultry, vegetables – anything you fancy can be used as a steamboat ingredient.

Serves 8–10

2 litres/3½ pints/9 cups boiling water
  (plus extra on the boil)
2 meat stock (bouillon) cubes

For the seasonings, dips and garnishes
a small bottle of light soy sauce
Chinese wine or sherry
6 garlic cloves, ground and fried until
  golden brown
6 spring onions (scallions), chopped
3–4 small dishes of chilli sauce
3–4 small dishes of black vinegar
ground black pepper

For the steamboat ingredients
250g/9oz tofu, cubed
450g/1lb chicken breast, thinly sliced
450g/1lb prawns (shrimp), shelled
30 prepared fish balls
4 pieces of fish cake
100g/3¾oz mung bean noodles, soaked
1 large Chinese cabbage,
  sliced into small pieces
50g/2oz golden needles (or dried lily
  buds), soaked and trimmed
200g/7oz pig's liver, thinly sliced

Per portion Energy 163kcal/687kJ; Protein 29g; Carbohydrate 3g, of which sugars 1g; Fat 4g, of which saturates 1g; Cholesterol 172mg; Calcium 200mg; Fibre 1g; Sodium 581mg.

Serves 4

450g/1lb prepared eel cutlets
45ml/3 tbsp vegetable oil
6 garlic cloves, sliced
3 spring onions (scallions),
  sliced into 5cm/2in lengths
15ml/1 tbsp black bean sauce
5ml/1 tsp sugar
15ml/1 tbsp Shaoxing wine
  or dry sherry
4 dried Chinese mushrooms,
  soaked and sliced
shredded lettuce, to serve

Cook's tip You can fry the eels lightly before using. This way, they hold their shape better during simmering.

Per portion Energy 324kcal/1344kJ; Protein 20g; Carbohydrate 6g, of which sugars 2g; Fat 24g, of which saturates 5g; Cholesterol 169mg; Calcium 38mg; Fibre 1g; Sodium 260mg.

Garlic fish

If you love garlic, this dish will soon be added to your treasure trove of fish dishes. In Hebei, garlic is used generously in dishes and is particularly suited to fish with strong flavours, such as mackerel and tuna steaks. In northern China the favoured fish is carp or eels. Eels are used in this dish because the aromatics enhance without overpowering the flavour of the fish. Always buy eels fresh and ask the fishmonger to gut and fillet them.

1 Wash and pat the eel pieces dry on kitchen paper. Heat the oil in a wok and fry the garlic until golden brown. Drain and set aside.

2 In the remaining oil, fry the spring onions for 1 minute, then add the black bean sauce, sugar, wine or sherry, and the mushrooms. Stir for 1 minute, then add 200ml/7fl oz/ scant 1 cup water.

3 Bring to the boil then add the eel and simmer for 10 minutes, or until well soused. Sprinkle fried garlic all over, then serve on a bed of shredded lettuce.

Trout in wine sauce

River trout are plentiful in the tributaries of northern China. In Jilin, the fish is often soused with plenty of wine, ginger and pungent bean sauces. Trout is a fish with a very subtle taste and it fries well. It has a slippery skin, but rubbing it vigorously with salt improves the texture. Instead of a whole fish, use fillets to save time (see Variation). A strong Chinese wine, such as kaoliang or rose-flavoured wine, will give the best flavour.

1 Rub the trout fillets with salt and rinse. Pat dry with kitchen paper, then coat with the cornflour. Heat the oil for deep-frying in a wok or deep-fryer. Deep-fry the fish until crisp, then set aside.

2 Heat the 15ml/1 tbsp oil in a wok and fry the garlic for 2 minutes. Add the sliced green pepper and spring onions, and fry for 1 minute.

3 Add the wine or sherry, sugar, sesame oil, pepper and 200ml/7fl oz/scant 1 cup water, and bring to the boil. Add the trout and simmer for about 3 minutes, until the fish is cooked through and the cornflour coating has thickened the sauce.

Variation You could also use trout fillets; you will need about 400g/14oz. Any other firm-fleshed fish fillets can be cooked in the same way.

Serves 4

2 large river trout
5ml/1 tsp salt
15ml/1 tbsp cornflour (cornstarch)
vegetable oil, for deep-frying
15ml/1 tbsp vegetable oil
4 garlic cloves, crushed
1 green (bell) pepper, thinly sliced
2 spring onions (scallions), white
 parts only, finely chopped
45ml/3 tbsp strong Chinese wine,
 such as kaoliang or rose-flavoured
 wine, or dry sherry
5ml/1 tsp sugar
15ml/1 tbsp sesame oil
2.5ml/½ tsp ground black pepper

Per portion Energy 300kcal/1251kJ; Protein 22g;
Carbohydrate 6g, of which sugars 2g; Fat 20g,
of which saturates 3g; Cholesterol 75mg;
Calcium 30mg; Fibre 1g; Sodium 546mg.

Braised fish in yellow bean sauce

Yellow bean sauce is a favourite seasoning in Chinese cooking, and it is often used in the north, where soya beans are widely grown and made into many kinds of sauces. Yellow bean sauce is less salty than black bean sauce, and it marries well with vinegar, sugar and pepper. Whole preserved yellow beans can be used instead of the sauce – crush them with a fork before using. Monkfish has a meaty texture, which lends itself to braising.

1 Cut the monkfish into medallions about 2cm/¾in thick. Heat the oil in a wok and shallow-fry for 3 minutes, turning once so that each piece is well sealed. Set aside.

2 In the remaining oil, fry the ginger for 2 minutes and add the pepper, yellow bean sauce and vinegar. Stir for 1 minute then add the fish, spring onions and 300ml/½ pint/1¼ cups water.

3 Simmer for 10 minutes, or until the sauce is slightly thick. If you prefer it thicker, blend the cornflour with water and add it to the sauce, then cook for 1 minute. Serve hot.

Variation Other firm-fleshed fish such as halibut, cod and snapper can be used in this dish, but you may need to reduce the cooking time.

Serves 4

450g/1lb monkfish tail, filleted and
  membrane removed
45ml/3 tbsp vegetable oil
25g/1oz fresh root ginger,
  peeled and grated
2.5ml/½ tsp ground black pepper
30ml/2 tbsp yellow bean sauce
15ml/1 tbsp rice vinegar
2 spring onions (scallions), chopped
5ml/1 tsp cornflour
  (cornstarch) (optional)

Per portion Energy 192kcal/805kJ; Protein 18g;
Carbohydrate 3g, of which sugars 1g; Fat 12g,
of which saturates 1g; Cholesterol 16mg;
Calcium 24mg; Fibre 1g; Sodium 211mg.

Serves 4

1 large whole carp, about 450g/1lb
5ml/1 tsp salt
25g/1oz cloud ear (wood ear)
  mushrooms, soaked until soft
vegetable oil, for deep-frying
25g/1oz fresh root ginger,
  peeled and grated
2 garlic cloves, crushed
15ml/1 tbsp chilli oil
30ml/2 tbsp rice vinegar
15ml/1 tbsp yellow bean sauce
2.5ml/½ tsp sugar
2 spring onions (scallions), chopped

Variation You can coat the whole fish in cornflour (cornstarch) before deep-frying to give it a crisp coating. When the sauce is hot, add the fish and simmer until cooked through. The cornflour will thicken the sauce.

Hot-and-sour carp

This recipe for carp creates a strongly flavoured Hebei dish that is typical of the province's cooking. The national capital of Beijing is situated within Hebei and this province is also where the massive Great Wall ends. Hebei is a mountainous plateau, traversed by tributaries of the Yellow River, which explains the area's fondness for freshwater fish.

1 Clean the carp but leave it whole. Make criss-cross cuts across the thickest part of the fish. Heat the oil for deep-frying in a wok or deep-fryer, then deep-fry the carp until crisp and cooked through. Set it aside and keep warm. Reserve 30ml/2 tbsp of the deep-frying oil.

2 Slice off and discard the woody parts from the cloud ears, then chop the fungus. In a wok, heat the reserved deep-frying oil, and fry the ginger and garlic for 2 minutes.

3 In a small bowl, blend the chilli oil with the vinegar, yellow bean sauce, sugar and 200ml/7fl oz/scant 1 cup water, then add it to the wok. Bring to the boil and add the cloud ears and spring onions. Cook for 1 minute, then pour over the fried fish. Serve immediately.

Carp in ginger and sesame sauce

The sesame sauce used in this Beijing dish is made from sesame paste, which is sold in all Chinese stores. Sesame paste has the same consistency as smooth peanut butter and it has a strong flavour. It blends well with aromatics like ginger or garlic. In this recipe, it gives the fish a subtle and slightly spicy flavour, accentuated by the dash of wine or sherry.

1 Clean the carp. Make diagonal cuts across the thickest part of the fish and rub the skin and cuts with salt. Heat the oil for deep-frying in a wok or deep-fryer, then deep-fry the carp until crisp and cooked through. Set it aside and keep warm.

2 Heat the 30ml/2 tbsp oil in a wok or frying pan and fry the ginger and garlic for 2 minutes. Add the sesame paste, wine or sherry, sugar and 200ml/7fl oz/scant 1 cup water, and bring to the boil.

3 Lower the fish into the wok or pan and simmer for 2 minutes, then turn it over once so that every part of the fish is bathed with the sauce. Serve hot, garnished with chopped spring onions.

Serves 4

1 large carp, about 450g/1lb
(head removed, if you like)
5ml/1 tsp salt
vegetable oil, for deep-frying,
plus 30ml/2 tbsp vegetable oil
25g/1oz fresh root ginger,
peeled and grated
3 garlic cloves, sliced
30ml/2 tbsp sesame paste
(*see* Cook's Tip) or tahini
15ml/1 tbsp Shaoxing wine
or dry sherry
2.5ml/½ tsp sugar
chopped spring onions (scallions),
to garnish

Cook's tip Make your own sesame paste by grinding 40g/1½oz sesame seeds until fine. Cook over low heat in 30ml/2 tbsp oil and a little water until a paste forms.

Per portion Energy 210kcal/873kJ; Protein 13g; Carbohydrate 2g, of which sugars 1g; Fat 16g, of which saturates 2g; Cholesterol 42mg; Calcium 99mg; Fibre 2g; Sodium 521mg.

Steamed fish with ginger

When fish is absolutely fresh, the best way to cook it is by steaming it with hints of ginger. A few pickled sour plums will heighten the subtle flavour of delicate fish such as sea bass, mullet or snapper, and a few shreds of salted mustard greens add a salty touch to the ensuing 'soup' that is created after steaming. This is a classic dish of Tianjin, a municipality that borders Hebei province and Beijing.

1 Pat the fish dry on kitchen paper, then make several deep cuts diagonally into the thickest part of each fish and place them into a deep plate or dish that will fit into your steamer.

2 Sprinkle the ginger all over the fish and put the sour plums on top. Add the salted mustard greens around the edge, tucking them in under the fish with a few shreds on top.

3 Drizzle the sesame oil and soy sauce all over, then sprinkle over the ground pepper. Sprinkle water along the sides of the plate or dish. Steam for 15 minutes, until cooked through. There will be a small amount of soup in the bottom of the plate or dish. Serve immediately.

Cook's tips
• The soup from this dish is delicious spooned over plain boiled rice.
• For special occasions, drizzle 30ml/1 tbsp cognac or brandy over the fish before serving.

Serves 4

2 whole sea bass, mullet or red
  snapper, cleaned
25g/1oz fresh root ginger,
  peeled and finely shredded
2 pickled sour plums
50g/2oz salted mustard greens,
  finely shredded
30ml/2 tbsp sesame oil
15ml/1 tbsp light soy sauce
2.5ml/½ tsp ground black pepper

Per portion Energy 161kcal/671kJ; Protein 15g; Carbohydrate 4g, of which sugars 3g; Fat 10g, of which saturates 1g; Cholesterol 60mg; Calcium 130mg; Fibre 1g; Sodium 278mg.

Crispy fish

Most northern fish dishes are bathed in a sauce; unadorned deep-fried fish is not common within the cuisine. There are exceptions, however, when the fish is of a superior quality and absolutely fresh. Even then, there is always a dip or two, or even a pouring sauce. Fish like snapper and tilapia are ideal for this Henan dish. This recipe has two dips, but you can serve the second dip as a sauce to pour over the fish instead, if you like.

1 To make the first dip, mince (grind) the ginger, garlic and spring onions until fine, then mix with the vinegar, yellow bean sauce, sugar, water and oil. Set aside in a small serving bowl.

2 To make the second dip or sauce, mix all the ingredients in a small pan and warm over gentle heat for 2 minutes. Set aside in another small serving bowl.

3 Snip off any protruding sharp fins from the fish, then coat in tapioca flour. Heat the oil for deep-frying in a wok or deep-fryer, then deep-fry the fish until golden brown. (You may need to do this one fish at a time.) Serve immediately, either with the two dips on the side or with the second dip poured over as a sauce.

Serves 4

2 whole snappers, about 450g/1lb
 total weight, cleaned
30ml/2 tbsp tapioca flour
vegetable oil, for deep-frying

For the first dip
25g/1oz fresh root ginger, peeled
3 garlic cloves
2 spring onions (scallions)
30ml/2 tbsp rice vinegar
15ml/1 tbsp yellow bean sauce
5ml/1 tsp sugar
45ml/3 tbsp warm water
5ml/1 tsp oil

For the second dip (or sauce)
15ml/1 tbsp plum sauce
15ml/1 tbsp rice vinegar
15ml/1 tbsp hoisin sauce
15ml/1 tbsp crushed garlic
45ml/3 tbsp warm water

Per portion Energy 197kcal/833kJ; Protein 31g;
Carbohydrate 11g, of which sugars 3g; Fat 3g,
of which saturates 1g; Cholesterol 56mg;
Calcium 67mg; Fibre 0g; Sodium 355mg.

Serves 4

450g/1lb snapper or grouper fillets
5ml/1 tsp cornflour (cornstarch),
  plus extra to coat
45ml/3 tbsp vegetable oil
3 garlic cloves, sliced
75g/3oz leeks, thinly sliced
30ml/2 tbsp Shaoxing wine
  or dry sherry
15ml/1 tbsp preserved red
  beancurd, mashed
15ml/1 tbsp hoisin sauce
15ml/1 tbsp rice vinegar
2.5ml/½ tsp sugar
5ml/1 tsp cornflour (cornstarch)
plain rice, to serve

Variation For a more traditional dish, deep-fry a whole fish, head and tail intact, and then pour the sauce over while the fish is still hot.

Per portion Energy 245kcal/1023kJ; Protein 23g; Carbohydrate 7g, of which sugars 2g; Fat 13g, of which saturates 2g; Cholesterol 42mg; Calcium 58mg; Fibre 1g; Sodium 279mg.

Red cooked fish

The technique of cooking seafood in a rich red sauce is typical of North China, especially Beijing. The colour is created through a mixture of hoisin sauce, preserved red beancurd and Shaoxing wine. This is a well-travelled dish and, in other regions, it takes on whatever indigenous ingredients are available. The term hong shao is also applied to many meat and poultry dishes that are cooked in a similar sauce to this.

1 Cut the fillets into bitesize pieces, then coat with cornflour. Heat the oil in a wok and shallow fry the fish pieces until they are cooked through and have a crisp coating. Set aside and keep warm.

2 In the remaining oil, fry the sliced garlic for 2 minutes, then add the leeks. Stir-fry for 1 minute. In a small bowl mix together the wine or sherry, preserved red beancurd, hoisin sauce, rice vinegar, sugar and 200ml/7fl oz/scant 1 cup water, then add it to the pan.

3 Cook, stirring, for 1 minute, then add the fish. Allow the fish to heat through for 30 seconds. Blend the teaspoonful of cornflour with a little water, and add to the pan. Stir for 1 minute, or until the sauce thickens, then serve hot, with rice.

Poultry

If there is one iconic dish to which Beijing can lay claim, it has to be Peking Duck, though this is by no means the only praiseworthy dish of the northern Chinese region. Many splendid chicken dishes have been enshrined in the culinary hall of fame. Northern chefs are skilled at coaxing glorious flavours from a selection of aromatics and wines, then marrying them with poultry. Most birds are steamed, fried or braised, and the artful use of wines and sauces brings out the sumptuous flavours of the meat.

Smoked, steamed and stir-fried

Symbolism is hugely important in Chinese culture, and it is particularly apparent in the culinary arts. Chicken is often inextricably linked with the mythical phoenix, and is a popular choice at Chinese New Year banquets and at weddings. Rich symbolism is displayed in the recipe known as Phoenix Chicken, the heraldic creature giving its name to the dish.

In the northern provinces, much use is made of smoking as a special technique, and chefs embrace the flavour imparted by tea leaves used as an aromatic smoking material.

Flavoursome ingredients like chestnuts, ginger and rice wine add many dimensions of taste to a humble chicken, duck or game bird. Kwei-Fei Chicken, commonly known as 'drunken chicken', is a firm favourite and a shining example of the northern love of poultry soused in plenty of wine.

While game is quite rare in much of China's provincial cooking, quail is a favourite bird in the rural northern areas. It is usually cooked in a marinade of wine, ginger, garlic and sesame oil, which lifts the taste of the bird to remarkable heights.

The most famous Mandarin dish has to be Peking Duck. Although the city is now known as Beijing, the older English spelling of Peking is preserved in the name of this age-old dish. Although the ingredients list is very short (just duck and Chinese maltose or clear honey), it takes a long time to prepare, and there are many restaurants in Beijing that specialize in this delicious dish.

Tea-smoked chicken

Not only is tea fundamental to Chinese cuisine, this beverage is also central to Chinese culture. Infusing foods with the delicate perfume of different teas is practised throughout the country, despite the complicated method involved. Five-star restaurants in major cities offer this dish, but it is within the reach of home cooks with some adaptation. What is important is the length of time needed to chill the seasoned chicken – about 2 hours. Semi-fermented oolong tea from the Fujian province gives the best flavour.

1 Rub the salt all over the breast of the chicken, then chill it for 2 hours.

2 Rinse the chicken thoroughly and pat it dry with kitchen paper. Cut down the breastbone to spatchcock the chicken, and press it down to flatten it out. Make several deep scores into the breast.

3 Line a large wok with a double sheet of foil. Mix the tea leaves with the flour, sugar and barley, and spread the mixture out evenly on top of the foil.

4 Place a bamboo steamer (large enough to take the chicken) over the top of the smoking materials so that there is space between the tea mixture and the steamer. Put the chicken directly on to the bamboo steamer and cover with the lid. Turn the heat to high and, when you see smoke emanating, adjust the heat so that there is no scorching. Smoke the chicken, covered, for 25 minutes, until cooked through, turning the chicken halfway through.

5 Transfer the chicken to a plate. Mix the wine or sherry, sesame oil and ginger in a bowl, then rub over the chicken. Leave to marinate for 15 minutes, then place in a steamer and steam for 1 hour, until fragrant. Serve immediately, with some noodles and fresh coriander, if you like.

Serves 4

5ml/1 tsp salt
1 whole chicken, about 1.5kg/3¼lb
45ml/3 tbsp Shaoxing wine
  or dry sherry
30ml/2 tbsp sesame oil
25g/1oz fresh root ginger, crushed
noodles, to serve
fresh coriander (cilantro), to garnish

For the smoking materials
50g/2oz tea leaves of your choice
150g/5oz/1¼ cups plain
  (all-purpose) flour
115g/4oz demerara (raw) sugar
75g/3oz barley

Per portion Energy 623kcal/2599kJ; Protein 57g; Carbohydrate 1g, of which sugars 0g; Fat 43g, of which saturates 12g; Cholesterol 258mg; Calcium 25mg; Fibre 0g; Sodium 673mg.

Smoked chicken

Smoking foods does not always involve tea – smoked seafoods, for example, are infused with the fragrance of different materials such as barley grains, Sichuan peppercorns, aromatic woods and pungent spices. It is a blank canvas, and you can create your own flavours for different foods. My particular favourite smoking materials for chicken are Sichuan peppercorns, cloves, cinnamon and coriander seeds, which mirror the Chinese five-spice powder in the marinade. This combination is a personal preference rather than a traditional one, but the method and resulting taste are quintessentially Chinese.

1 Rub the salt all over the chicken breasts, then chill them for 15 minutes.

2 Rinse the chicken thoroughly and pat it dry with kitchen paper. Make a few gashes into the thickest part and rub with soy sauce and wine or sherry.

3 Line a large wok with a double sheet of foil. Mix the cloves with the cinnamon, flour, sugar and coriander seeds, then spread the mixture evenly on top of the foil. Put a bamboo steamer in the wok. It should be large enough to hold the chicken on top while leaving space between the smoking mixture and the steamer.

4 Put the chicken directly on to the bamboo steamer and cover with the lid. Turn the heat to high and, when you see smoke emanating, adjust the heat so that there is no scorching. Smoke the chicken, covered, for 15 minutes, until partially cooked, turning the chicken halfway through.

5 Transfer the chicken to a plate. Mix the garlic, Chinese five-spice powder and sesame oil in a bowl, and rub this mixture over the chicken. Leave to marinate for 15 minutes, then place in a steamer over boiling water, and steam for 20 minutes, until fragrant. Slice and serve, garnished with shredded spring onions and accompanied by a chilli sauce dip.

Serves 4

5ml/1 tsp salt
2 skinless chicken breasts
15ml/1 tbsp soy sauce
30ml/2 tbsp Shaoxing wine
 or dry sherry
3 garlic cloves, crushed
a pinch of Chinese five-spice powder
15ml/1 tbsp sesame oil
shredded spring onion (scallion),
 to garnish
chilli sauce dip, to serve

For the smoking materials
15 cloves
2 sticks cinnamon, broken into
 small pieces
150g/5oz/1¼ cups plain
 (all-purpose) flour
115g/4oz demerara (raw) sugar
15ml/1 tbsp coriander seeds

Variation Replace the smoking materials with a selection of herbs, such as thyme, lavender and rosemary.

Per portion Energy 126kcal/529kJ; Protein 18g; Carbohydrate 1g, of which sugars 0g; Fat 5g, of which saturates 1g; Cholesterol 53mg; Calcium 6mg; Fibre 0g; Sodium 716mg.

Chicken with walnuts

Serves 4

115g/4oz/1 cup walnuts
15ml/1 tbsp vegetable oil
3 garlic cloves, sliced
400g/14oz skinless chicken breast,
  cut into 1cm/½in cubes
5ml/1 tsp sugar
5ml/1 tsp rice vinegar
15ml/1 tbsp Chinese maltose or
  clear honey
15ml/1 tbsp yellow bean sauce
shredded lettuce, to serve

Variation You can replace the
walnuts with diced carrots, celery
or water chestnuts, if you like.

*Although they do not appear often in Chinese cooking, walnuts are a
particular favourite of the northern regions, as they are farmed widely here.
The indentations in walnuts make an attractive contrast to the smoothness
of sliced chicken, and they soak up the rich yellow bean sauce beautifully.
This Shandong dish has influenced the cuisine of Guangzhou, where
chicken is fried with cashew nuts. This is a fairly sweet dish because of the
inclusion of Chinese maltose, which is normally used as a rub for Peking
duck. Use clear honey if this is unavailable.*

1 Wash and drain the walnuts, removing any excess skins. Heat the oil in a wok and fry the
garlic for 2 minutes, or until golden brown.

2 Add the chicken and stir-fry for 2 minutes. Add the walnuts and sugar, then stir-fry until
the walnuts are slightly caramelized.

3 Add the rice vinegar, maltose or honey, yellow bean sauce and 75ml/5 tbsp water,
then stir vigorously until the sauce is thick and the chicken and walnuts are well coated.
Serve immediately, on a bed of shredded lettuce.

Per portion Energy 359kcal/1459kJ; Protein 29g;
Carbohydrate 6g, of which sugars 5g; Fat 25g,
of which saturates 2g; Cholesterol 70mg;
Calcium 36mg; Fibre 2g; Sodium 157mg.

Chicken with hoisin sauce

From Henan comes a dish that uses hoisin sauce (also called sweet bean sauce) to wonderful effect. Many northern chefs make their own hoisin sauce by blending yellow bean sauce with sugar until the correct level of sweetness is achieved. For this dish, you can choose the complementary ingredient to work with the chicken – water chestnuts, ginkgo nuts, lotus seeds or lychees – all of which will give delicious results.

1 Cut the water chestnuts, ginkgo nuts, lotus seeds or lychees into bitesize pieces. Heat the oil in a wok, add the onion and stir-fry for 3 minutes.

2 Add the chicken and stir-fry for 2 minutes. Add the hoisin sauce, black pepper and rice vinegar, and cook, stirring, for 2 minutes.

3 Blend 90ml/6 tbsp water with the cornflour, and add to the wok. Stir until the sauce has thickened slightly. Serve immediately, garnished with coriander leaves and accompanied by plain boiled rice.

Serves 4

150g/5oz water chestnuts, ginkgo
    nuts, lotus seeds or lychees
    (*see* Cook's Tip)
15ml/1 tbsp vegetable oil
½ large onion, sliced or chopped
400g/14oz skinless chicken breast,
    cut into 1cm/½in cubes
30ml/2 tbsp hoisin sauce
2.5ml/½ tsp ground black pepper
15ml/1 tbsp rice vinegar
5ml/1 tsp cornflour (cornstarch)
fresh coriander (cilantro), to garnish
plain boiled rice, to serve

Cook's tip If you are using canned lychees, add 15–30ml/1–2 tbsp lychee juice to the sauce for extra fragrance.

Per portion Energy 178kcal/751kJ; Protein 25g;
Carbohydrate 8g, of which sugars 4g; Fat 5g,
of which saturates 1g; Cholesterol 70mg;
Calcium 21mg; Fibre 2g; Sodium 254mg.

Phoenix chicken

The heraldic phoenix is an important symbol that permeates the entire Chinese culture because of its connection to rebirth, and it is often associated with chicken. Dim sum restaurant menus usually advertise chicken feet as 'phoenix claws', and I have amusing recollections of unwary Western friends ordering what they thought was a grand delicacy and receiving chicken feet! This dish is fragrant with ginger.

1 Trim off any excess fat or protruding bones from the chicken pieces, then rub the chicken with the salt.

2 Heat 30ml/2 tbsp of the oil in a wok, add the chicken and shallow-fry it for 5 minutes, turning constantly until every piece is well sealed and the chicken skin shrinks a little. Remove the chicken pieces from the wok and set aside.

3 Clean the wok and heat the remaining oil. Fry the garlic and ginger for 2 minutes. Add the black bean sauce, sugar and pepper, and cook for 1 minute.

4 Return the chicken to the wok and add 250ml/8fl oz/1 cup water. Cook over high heat for 5 minutes, then add the leek.

5 Continue to cook over a high heat until the sauce is reduced by half. Blend the cornflour with a little water, and add to the sauce. Stir and cook for a further 2 minutes, until the chicken is cooked through and the sauce is thickened. Serve hot.

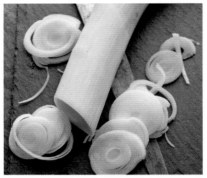

Serves 4

1 whole chicken, about 1.5kg/3¼lb, cut into 8 large joints
5ml/1 tsp salt
45ml/3 tbsp vegetable oil
3 garlic cloves, sliced
40g/1½oz fresh root ginger, peeled and grated
15ml/1 tbsp black bean sauce
5ml/1 tsp sugar
2.5ml/½ tsp ground black pepper
1 leek, finely sliced
15ml/1 tbsp cornflour (cornstarch)

Variations Other sauces can be used instead of black bean sauce to create different flavours: try plum sauce for a slightly sweet hint or oyster sauce for a more savoury finish.

Per portion Energy 466kcal/1947kJ; Protein 52g; Carbohydrate 7g, of which sugars 2g; Fat 26g, of which saturates 5g; Cholesterol 197mg; Calcium 31mg; Fibre 1g; Sodium 739mg.

Serves 4

4 chicken legs (or 4 chicken thighs
 and 4 chicken drumsticks)
5ml/1 tsp salt
30ml/2 tbsp strong Chinese wine
 or sherry
15ml/1 tbsp cornflour (cornstarch)
vegetable oil, for deep-frying
sliced pineapple or cucumber,
 to serve

For the sauce
30ml/2 tbsp hoisin sauce
45ml/3 tbsp pineapple juice
15ml/1 tbsp rice vinegar
15ml/1 tbsp light soy sauce
120ml/4fl oz/½ cup water
15ml/1 tbsp cornflour (cornstarch)

Cook's tip Pour the sauce over the
chicken just before serving to retain
the crispness of the chicken.

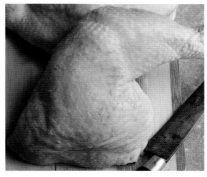

Per portion Energy 202kcal/839kJ; Protein 9g;
Carbohydrate 9g, of which sugars 2g; Fat 14g,
of which saturates 2g; Cholesterol 48mg;
Calcium 13mg; Fibre 0g; Sodium 899mg.

Oil-soaked chicken

*This classic Beijing dish actually originated in Fujian – it was probably poached
by visiting emperors from the capital city. Although the name might imply
greasiness, it simply means that the chicken has been deep-fried after an
initial steaming step. This 'twice-cooked' method is commonly employed by
Chinese chefs, and the result is an incredibly crisp yet succulent bird,
bathed in a heady wine sauce. It is almost like a sweet-and-sour dish.*

1 Cut each chicken leg into two joints (thigh and drumstick), then rub them all over with the
salt and wine or sherry. Place them into a steamer and steam for 15 minutes, until partially
cooked. Set them aside to cool.

2 When the chicken is cool enough to handle, coat each piece liberally with cornflour. Heat
the oil for deep-frying, and deep-fry the chicken pieces for 8 minutes, or until golden brown
and cooked through. Remove and keep warm.

3 To make the sauce, blend the hoisin sauce with the pineapple juice, vinegar, soy sauce,
water and cornflour in a wok, and stir well. Bring the sauce to a gentle boil.

4 Pour the sauce over the chicken and serve immediately, with sliced pineapple or cucumber.

Serves 4

1 whole chicken, about 1.5kg/3¼lb
  (or 450g/1lb joints or breasts)
plain noodles or rice, to serve

For the marinade
30ml/2 tbsp Shaoxing wine
  or dry sherry
30ml/2 tbsp light soy sauce
15ml/1 tbsp sesame oil
2.5ml/½ tsp ground black pepper
2 spring onions (scallions), cut in half
15ml/1 tbsp ginger purée
15ml/1 tbsp garlic purée

Cook's tip You can add a few tablespoonfuls of water to the chicken when it steams, if you like, to give you a delicious, light soup at the end which you can serve alongside the chicken to moisten the noodles or rice, and to give extra fragrance.

Steamed chicken with wine

This is a northern Chinese favourite that has transcended the borders, and even the seas – steamed chicken with wine is now a staple in just about every Chinese home, wherever it may be. It is a simple dish, even for novice cooks – if you have all the ingredients, all you do is sit and watch it steam. The delectable results belie the simplicity of preparation. A whole chicken is used here, but you can use joints or breasts, if you prefer.

1 If using a whole chicken, cut down the breastbone to spatchcock the chicken, and press it down to flatten it out. Put all the marinade ingredients into a deep bowl (big enough to take the chicken) and mix well.

2 Add the chicken and cover it with the marinade, then leave for 15 minutes. Transfer the chicken to a deep plate or ceramic dish that will fit into your steamer. Spread the spring onions from the marinade on top.

3 Steam, covered, for 1 hour, or until cooked through. Serve with plain rice or noodles, and with any liquid left in the bottom of the plate, if you like (*see* Cook's Tip).

Per portion Energy 173kcal/727kJ; Protein 28g; Carbohydrate 2g, of which sugars 1g; Fat 5g, of which saturates 1g; Cholesterol 79mg; Calcium 16mg; Fibre 0g; Sodium 427mg.

Kwei-fei chicken

Commonly called 'drunken chicken', this is a Beijing classic. Yang Kwei-Fei was an empress of the Tang Dynasty in the 7th century, noted not only for her beauty but also for her fondness for a tipple. If legend is to be believed, she was known to instruct her palace chefs to souse chicken with huge quantities of wine. As a final touch, you can add some sliced mushrooms to the casserole during the last 5 minutes of cooking.

1 Wash the chicken, then pat it dry with kitchen paper. Rub all over inside and out with 15ml/ 1 tbsp each of the Shaoxing wine or sherry, and the light soy sauce. Set aside for 20 minutes.

2 Heat the oil for deep-frying in a wok, and deep-fry the chicken until the skin takes on a crisp, golden-brown hue. Lift out the chicken and drain. Boil a large pan of water, and blanch the chicken for 4 minutes, then drain again.

3 Transfer to a deep pan or wok with the remaining wine, sherry or port, soy sauce whole spring onions and salt.

4 Add the stock cube and about 1.2 litres/2 pints/5 cups water, or enough to ensure that it just covers the chicken. Simmer, covered, for 1½ hours, turning once or twice. By then the meat should just fall off the bones. Serve hot.

Serves 4

1 whole chicken, about 1.5kg/3¼lb
120ml/4fl oz/½ cup Shaoxing wine
  or dry sherry
45ml/3 tbsp light soy sauce
vegetable oil, for deep-frying
45ml/3 tbsp port
4 spring onions (scallions)
2.5ml/½ tsp salt
1 chicken stock (bouillon) cube

Cook's tip

How much water you will need depends on the size of your pan. The cardinal rule is to use a pan that just cradles the bird. Most Chinese chefs prefer to slow-cook in a wok, as the curved shape is ideal for this.

Per portion Energy 534kcal/2225kJ; Protein 44g; Carbohydrate 2g, of which sugars 1g; Fat 34g, of which saturates 9g; Cholesterol 193mg; Calcium 36mg; Fibre 0g; Sodium 1216mg.

Braised chicken and chestnuts

This all-time favourite combination of flavours can also be used with duck, but chicken is equally tasty and it takes half the time to cook. The floury texture and sweetness of chestnuts complements chicken superbly. Chestnuts are commonly sold canned or vacuum-packed. Raw chestnuts are time-consuming and fiddly to prepare, with only a slight difference in taste, though you can use raw chesnuts, if you like (see Cook's Tip).

1 Remove the skin from the chicken thighs and cut each thigh in half. Heat the vegetable oil in a wok, add the garlic and stir-fry for 2 minutes, or until golden brown.

2 Add the sesame oil and the chicken, and stir-fry for 2 minutes, or until the chicken is sealed all over. Add the chestnuts, spring onions, hoisin sauce, oyster sauce and preserved red beancurd, and cook, stirring vigorously, for 2 minutes, until well blended.

3 Add 200ml/7fl oz/scant 1 cup water and bring to the boil. Simmer for 20 minutes, or until the sauce is very thick and the chicken pieces are cooked through.

Serves 4

450g/1lb boneless chicken thighs
30ml/2 tbsp vegetable oil
3 garlic cloves, chopped
15ml/1 tbsp sesame oil
20 cooked and peeled chestnuts,
  canned or vacuum-packed
  (*see* Cook's Tip)
2 spring onions (scallions), chopped
15ml/1 tbsp hoisin sauce
30ml/2 tbsp oyster sauce
1 cube preserved red
  beancurd, mashed

Cook's tip If you prefer to prepare your own chestnuts, soak them overnight, then boil for 15 minutes. Cool and remove the skins – this is fiddly, as the skins are buried in the crevices of each nut.

Per portion Energy 296kcal/1216kJ; Protein 24g; Carbohydrate 8g, of which sugars 3g; Fat 19g, of which saturates 4g; Cholesterol 114mg; Calcium 30mg; Fibre 2g; Sodium 479mg.

4 prepared quails

15ml/1 tbsp dark soy sauce

30ml/2 tbsp vegetable oil

3 garlic cloves, chopped

25oz/1 oz fresh root ginger,
  peeled and chopped

15ml/1 tbsp sesame oil

30ml/2 tbsp oyster sauce

15ml/1 tbsp Chinese wine or sherry

5ml/1 tsp sugar

5ml/1 tsp ground black pepper

15ml/1 tbsp cornflour (cornstarch)

Cook's tip If you deep-fry the marinated quails briefly, it will shorten the simmering time and also result in the skin having a crispier texture.

Per portion Energy 550kcal/293kJ; Protein 49g; Carbohydrate 16g, of which sugars 3g; Fat 32g, of which saturates 5g; Cholesterol 44mg; Calcium 70mg; Fibre 0g; Sodium 1185mg.

Braised quails

Game birds are more popular in China's rural north (where quail, partridge and other wild birds thrive) than they are in towns. Quails, however, often appear on banquet menus today. They are very small birds and you need two for an adult main course portion or one as an appetizer. The important thing to remember with game is that the meat is quite dry and needs slow cooking to moisten and tenderize it. Braising does this perfectly.

1 Wash the quails, then pat them dry with kitchen paper. Rub them with the dark soy sauce. Heat the oil in a wok, add the garlic and ginger, and stir-fry for 2 minutes, or until golden.

2 Add the sesame oil, oyster sauce, wine or sherry, sugar and pepper, and cook, stirring, for 1 minute. Add the quails and cook, turning them a few times, for 3 minutes.

3 Add 500ml/17fl oz/2¼ cups water and cook over high heat for 20 minutes, or until the sauce is slightly reduced. Blend the cornflour with a little water and add to the wok to thicken the sauce. If you like your quails a little pink, they should be ready to serve now; if you like them more well-done, continue cooking until cooked through.

4 Serve the quails hot, with the sauce poured over, accompanied by plain rice.

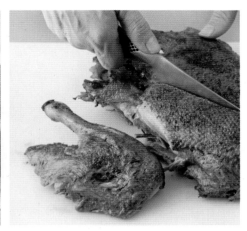

Braised duck in peppery soy sauce

The sauce in this dish is similar to the southern Chinese pork dish called Mists of Harmony, which uses caramelized dark soy sauce and pepper. As duck is richer than pork, here the fattiness is cut with pepper and cloves. It does take time to cook, but is well worth the effort. If you have a pressure cooker, this will take about half the time to cook and requires half the quantity of water. Use the thickest dark soy sauce you can find; the variety labelled sweet soy sauce (kecap manis in Indonesian) is excellent.

Serves 6–8

1 oven-ready duck
5ml/1 tsp salt
30ml/2 tbsp vegetable oil
15ml/1 tbsp sugar
75ml/5 tbsp dark soy sauce
5ml/1 tsp Chinese five-spice powder
10ml/2 tsp ground black pepper
6 cloves
2 thumb-sized pieces of fresh root ginger, peeled and bruised
chilli and garlic sauce, sliced cucumber and plain boiled rice, to serve

1 Wash the duck and pat it dry with kitchen paper, then rub salt all over the duck, inside and out. Heat the oil in the largest wok you have and caramelize the sugar until it froths and turns a dark brown.

2 Roll the duck in the sugar, turning over once or twice until the skin is coated in the sugar. Add the soy sauce and continue to cook, bathing the duck in it, for 3 minutes.

3 Add the remaining ingredients and 2 litres/3½ pints/9 cups water, and bring to the boil. Transfer to a deep, high-sided pan and simmer the duck, covered, for at least 2 hours, checking regularly to see if you need to top up with hot water.

4 When the duck is tender, remove it from the sauce. Turn up the heat and boil to reduce the sauce by about half. Allow the duck to cool enough so that you can chop it into smaller pieces or debone it, then serve it with a sharp chilli and garlic sauce, and sliced cucumber. Serve the reduced sauce on the side with plain rice.

Cook's tips

• If you prefer, you can thicken the sauce by stirring in 15ml/1 tbsp cornflour blended with water, then cook for 2 minutes.
• If you make this dish the day before, chill the sauce overnight. The next day the duck fat will have solidified on the top. Remove this for a lighter sauce, and reheat the duck to serve.

Per portion Energy 657kcal/2719kJ; Protein 31g; Carbohydrate 1g, of which sugars 0g; Fat 59g, of which saturates 17g; Cholesterol 149mg; Calcium 35mg; Fibre 0g; Sodium 917mg.

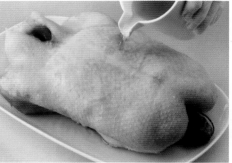

Peking duck

If ever there was a dish that won international plaudits, this is the one. It is completely different from crispy aromatic duck, which hails from Sichuan province and is often confused with its Beijing cousin. Why the name has never been changed to Beijing Duck is purely due to tradition. Few restaurants outside of China serve true Peking Duck, as it requires around 48 hours of preparation and does not lend itself to short-order cooking, unlike the Sichuan recipe. Regardless, it is worth all the effort. Many restaurants in Beijing specialize in nothing but this dish, and it is served over a three-course meal – duck with pancakes, stir-fried duck with vegetables and, lastly, the meaty carcass goes into the kitchen to emerge as a soup to finish the meal.

1 A day or two before serving, wipe the duck dry with kitchen paper both inside and out and hang it in a warm place to dry overnight or for up to 2 days.

2 On the morning of roasting, use a hair-dryer to thoroughly dry the duck skin all over. This will result in really crispy skin that pops away from the meat when you carve the duck. Boil a kettleful of water. Put the duck in a large colander and pour boiling water all over and inside the duck. Do this twice so that the duck skin shrinks and some fat is removed.

3 Melt the honey or maltose in a pan and add 200ml/7fl oz/scant 1 cup water. Bathe the duck with this mixture, then leave it to dry for at least 6 hours.

4 Preheat the oven to 200°C/400°F/Gas 6. Put the duck on a rack in a roasting pan and roast for 1¼ hours. The duck meat should still be a little pink; do not overcook.

5 Meanwhile, put the hoisin sauce into several small sauce dishes and arrange the spring onions and cucumber on small serving plates on the table. Lightly steam each stack of 8 pancakes for 3 minutes. Carve the duck, taking away squares or strips of skin and meat. Each diner then spreads a pancake with a little hoisin sauce, tops it with spring onions and cucumber, adds some Peking duck, and rolls the pancake up to eat.

Serves 8

1 oven-ready duck
30ml/2 tbsp Chinese maltose or
  clear honey

To serve
24 Mandarin pancakes (*see* recipe
  page 112–13, or use store-bought)
hoisin sauce
5 spring onions (scallions), sliced
  very finely into 5cm/2in strips
½ cucumber, peeled and sliced very
  finely into 5cm/2in strips

Cook's tips
• Mandarin pancakes are sold frozen in Chinese stores. They can be microwaved individually for 10 seconds.
• Any leftover duck can be shredded and stir-fried with vegetables.
• Boil the carcass in a large pan of water to use as a stock or for soup.

Per portion Energy 113kcal/476kJ; Protein 13g; Carbohydrate 3g, of which sugars 3g; Fat 6g, of which saturates 2g; Cholesterol 63mg; Calcium 8mg; Fibre 0g; Sodium 54mg.

Meat

Throughout much of China's history, particularly until the last few decades of industrial development, most people from the rural northern provinces could not afford meat on a daily basis. It was this scarcity that led to chefs and cooks using their culinary ingenuity to create thrifty dishes. While the menus of much of China are made up almost entirely of pork, the northern region has long been home to sheep and goat herds, which add a different dimension to the menu. While pork is used in many recipes, it is the lamb recipes of the region that have become famous around the world.

Hearty stews and warming spices

While Chinese city-dwellers today have the privilege of buying meat at large wet markets or modern supermarkets, many people in rural northern China depend on local butchers or their own small herds. With poverty still widespread in these areas, many of the cuts of meat available to locals are the cheaper, tougher cuts. This explains why many dishes are marinated with wine, bean sauces and aromatics, and stewed until fork-tender.

Being China's favourite meat, pork features on the menu in the form of perfectly cooked Stewed Spare Ribs, which have earned their cachet world-wide, and Mu Shu Pork, which has become a signature dish in just about every Chinese restaurant around the globe.

Lamb and mutton are put to excellent use in northern Chinese cookery. Locally, the word mutton is often used to refer to goat meat, rather than to meat from older sheep, though goat can be difficult to get hold of and mutton can work just as well.

Offal (variety meats) like liver and kidney get special treatment with wine and herbs, cutting their strong flavours. Spices like cumin, caraway, cloves and pepper have been employed by chefs in the region for hundreds of years, as they have been available there since the first century.

This is a region that is home to many Chinese Muslims, for example the Uyghur peoples of Xinjiang, who eschew the eating of pork. Lamb, mutton, goat and beef are their meat mainstays, another reason why they have become quintessential to the cuisine.

500g/1¼lb spare ribs,
  cut into 5cm/2in lengths
15ml/1 tbsp vegetable oil
3 garlic cloves, crushed
25g/1oz fresh root ginger, grated

For the marinade
30ml/2 tbsp dark soy sauce
5ml/1 tsp sugar
30ml/2 tbsp oyster sauce
30ml/2 tbsp Shaoxing wine
  or dry sherry
30ml/2 tbsp plum sauce
2.5ml/½ tsp ground black pepper
a pinch of Chinese five-spice powder
shredded spring onion (scallion),
  to garnish

Cook's tip If you want really tender ribs, add 5ml/1 tsp bicarbonate of soda (baking soda) to the marinade. When you add them to the wok, there will be a little froth, but it will subside after a few seconds.

Stewed spare ribs

With pork as the most popular meat throughout China, there is never any shortage of spare ribs cut in precisely the way they should be, with every rib having the perfect ratio of lean meat to fat. The best way to coax maximum succulence from them is to braise or stew them in a rich seasoning; deep-frying them, as many restaurants tend to do, can render them quite dry. If you marinate them for a few hours, they will be ambrosial.

1 Combine all the marinade ingredients in a large bowl, add the ribs and coat them well in the marinade. Leave to marinate for 4–6 hours or overnight.

2 Heat the oil in a wok, add the garlic and ginger, and stir-fry for 2 minutes. Add 450ml/¾ pint/scant 2 cups water, the ribs and all the marinade, and cook, stirring, for 2 minutes.

3 Transfer all the contents to a pan with a tight-fitting lid and bring to the boil. Cook over high heat for 15 minutes, then turn down to medium heat and simmer for 40 minutes, until the sauce is very thick and glossy. Serve hot, garnished with shredded spring onion.

Per portion Energy 301kcal/1250kJ; Protein 24g; Carbohydrate 6g, of which sugars 3g; Fat 19g, of which saturates 6g; Cholesterol 84mg; Calcium 16mg; Fibre 0g; Sodium 820mg.

Pork and turnips

Like other root vegetables, turnips are used in numerous ways in Chinese cuisine: boiled, steamed, mashed, dried and pickled. Chopped and salted turnips are a perennial favourite garnish in most Chinese regional cuisines – imparting a salty and smoky tang to congee, soups and stir-fries. When simply stir-fried, they have a delightful crunch with a subtle, sweet flavour. Swede (rutababa) can also be used instead of turnip.

1 Remove the skin from the leg of pork and slice the meat into thin strips. Rub salt all over the turnips and set them aside to sweat for 20 minutes. Squeeze handfuls of turnip to remove as much moisture as possible. This is will ensure that they retain their crunch.

2 Heat the oil in a wok, add the garlic and stir-fry for 2 minutes. Add the pork strips and continue to stir-fry vigorously for 2–3 minutes.

3 Add the black bean sauce, sesame oil and sugar, and stir-fry for 1 minute. Add 120ml/ 4fl oz/½ cup water and bring to a brisk boil. Stir for 3 minutes, or until the pork is nearly cooked and turning opaque.

4 Add the turnip and cook, stirring, for 2 minutes, until the pork and turnips are cooked through. Serve hot with noodles or rice.

Serves 4

450g/1lb boneless leg of pork
5ml/1 tsp salt
150g/5oz turnip, cut into
  bitesize pieces
15ml/1 tbsp vegetable oil
2 garlic cloves, crushed
30ml/2 tbsp black bean sauce
15ml/1 tbsp sesame oil
5ml/1 tsp sugar
noodles or plain boiled rice, to serve

Variation Root vegetables, such as carrots or mooli (daikon), can be used instead of turnip, for a tasty alternative.

Per portion Energy 210kcal/880kJ; Protein 25g;
Carbohydrate 4g, of which sugars 4g; Fat10g,
of which saturates 2g; Cholesterol 72mg;
Calcium 32mg; Fibre 1g; Sodium 758mg.

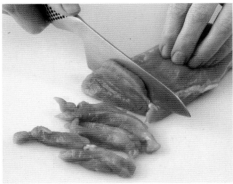

Mu shu pork

Also known as 'egg flower pork', this dish plays an important role as a filling for pancake rolls and other northern breads in Mandarin cooking. Mu shu is the name for the dried lily buds, or golden needles, that are integral to the dish, together with cloud ear mushrooms. The name also reflects the hint of gold in the eggs that are added. This is a time-honoured dish that is featured on the menus of restaurants within and beyond China.

1 Cut the pork into thin strips, each about 6cm/2½in long. Mix the marinade ingredients together in a shallow dish, then add the pork and mix to coat all the pork thoroughly. Marinate for 15 minutes.

2 Heat half the vegetable oil in a wok, add the pork and stir-fry for 3 minutes, until it is sealed all over and almost cooked through. Transfer the pork to a heatproof bowl and set aside.

3 Add a little more oil to the wok, if needed, then add the cloud ear mushrooms and golden needles, and stir-fry for 1 minute.

4 Add the soy sauces and sugar, and cook, stirring, for 1 minute. Transfer the mixture to the heatproof bowl containing the pork.

5 Clean the wok and add a little more oil. Add the eggs and stir (as you would for scrambled eggs) until they start to solidify. Add the chives, wine or sherry, and sesame oil, and cook, stirring, for 1 minute.

6 Add the fried pork, cloud ears and golden needles, then continue to cook, stirring, for 1–2 minutes, until the pork is cooked through and everything is well incorporated. Serve with plain rice.

Cook's tip The different ingredients are partly cooked, then combined at the end so that they will cook evenly.

Variation This pork dish can also be used as a filling for Mandarin pancakes.

Serves 4

350g/12oz lean pork with a little fat
about 120ml/4fl oz/½ cup vegetable oil
25g/1oz cloud ear (wood ear)
  mushrooms, soaked until soft
25g/1oz golden needles,
  soaked and trimmed
15ml/1 tbsp light soy sauce
15ml/1 tbsp dark soy sauce
2.5ml/½ tsp sugar
4 eggs, lightly beaten
10 Chinese yellow chives,
  cut into 5cm/2in lengths
15ml/1 tbsp Shaoxing wine
  or dry sherry
15ml/1 tbsp sesame oil
plain boiled rice, to serve

For the marinade
2.5ml/½ tsp salt
5ml/1 tsp light soy sauce
2.5ml/½ tsp ground black pepper
15ml/1 tbsp Shaoxing wine
  or dry sherry
5ml/1 tsp cornflour (cornstarch)
30ml/2 tbsp water

Per portion Energy 540kcal/2239kJ; Protein 28g; Carbohydrate 10g, of which sugars 1g; Fat 43g, of which saturates 7g; Cholesterol 288mg; Calcium 53mg; Fibre 0g; Sodium 384mg.

Sweet-and-sour lamb

Although lamb is not normally associated with sweet-and-sour flavours, this is popular in Shanxi province among the Chinese Muslims who do not eat pork. The origin of 'sweet-and-sour' is usually attributed to Shanghai chefs, though northerners refute this, claiming it to be an invention of palace chefs in the Forbidden City. No one knows for sure, but every chef worth his soy sauce has his own version. The dish is truly iconic today, whether it is cooked with pork, chicken or shellfish. The juxtaposition of these two flavours reflects the yin-yang philosophy of perfect balance.

1 Coat the lamb cubes with cornflour. Heat the oil for deep-frying in a wok or deep-fryer, and deep-fry the lamb until golden brown and cooked through. Set aside.

2 In a clean wok, heat the 30ml/2 tbsp oil, add the ginger and garlic, and stir-fry for 1 minute. Add the quartered onion, and fry for 2 minutes, or until soft and the onion layers separate.

3 Blend the yellow bean sauce with the sugar, plum sauce and 200ml/7fl oz/scant 1 cup water, then add to the pan. Bring to the boil, then add the fried lamb. Simmer for 2–3 minutes, or until well incorporated and the sauce is glossy and thick. Serve hot.

Variation Ring the changes and add other ingredients such as carrots, mushrooms, or even lychees, to bulk up the dish. To strike a proper balance, use about 75g/3oz of each vegetable or fruit and the dish will feed up to six people.

Serves 4

300g/11oz lean lamb, cut into
  1cm/½in cubes
15ml/1 tbsp cornflour (cornstarch)
vegetable oil, for deep-frying
30ml/2 tbsp vegetable oil
15ml/1 tbsp sliced fresh root ginger
15ml/1 tbsp sliced garlic
1 large onion, quartered
15ml/1 tbsp yellow bean sauce
15ml/1 tbsp sugar
15ml/1 tbsp plum sauce

Per portion Energy 243kcal/1014kJ; Protein 17g; Carbohydrate 14g, of which sugars 9g; Fat 14g, of which saturates 3g; Cholesterol 56mg; Calcium 30mg; Fibre 1g; Sodium 151mg.

Serves 4

200g/7oz lamb fillet
3 eggs, lightly beaten
15ml/1 tbsp fresh root ginger, grated
15ml/1 tbsp lard, white cooking fat
    or vegetable oil
15ml/1 tbsp Shaoxing wine
    or dry sherry
15ml/1 tbsp light soy sauce
2.5ml/½ tsp ground black pepper
shredded spring onion (scallion),
    to garnish
plain boiled rice or steamed bread,
    to serve

Cook's tip A pair of chopsticks, with the aid of your wok ladle, will break up and scramble the eggs as they should be.

Per portion Energy 210kcal/873kJ; Protein 16g; Carbohydrate 1g, of which sugars 0g; Fat 16g, of which saturates 6g; Cholesterol 215mg; Calcium 31mg; Fibre 0g; Sodium 274mg.

Cassia lamb

The evergreen tree cassia is indigenous to southern China and South-east Asia. It has tiny, yellow flowers with four petals, and it has a close relative, known as 'true cinnamon', which is primarily used for its aromatic bark. In fact, there is neither cassia nor cinnamon in this dish – the name alludes to the colour of the cooked eggs only. Such is Chinese symbolism that the recipe name can tell an entirely different story from the ingredients list!

1 Cut the lamb into thin strips and tenderize it with a meat mallet or the blunt edge of a cleaver until it is almost shredded. Place the lamb in a bowl, add the eggs and ginger, and mix well.

2 Heat the lard, white cooking fat or oil in a wok, add the lamb mixture and stir-fry over high heat for 1 minute, or until the eggs are scrambled.

3 Add the wine or sherry, soy sauce and pepper, and cook, stirring, for 1 minute more. The dish will have a distinct yellow hue. Garnish with shredded spring onions and serve with rice or steamed bread.

Cumin and caraway lamb

Spices have been used in northern Chinese cooking for centuries. After all, the silk and spice routes were opened as far back as the 1st century BC, and spices like cumin, caraway, pepper, cloves and cinnamon were traded like precious stones. The Uyghur people in Xinjiang (who are predominantly Muslim) and the nomadic Mongols have been using spices in their cooking for a long time. Collectively, they are known as the Hui, and they may speak Chinese but are affiliated to the Sunni branch of Islam.

1 Cut the lamb into thin strips and rub them with the cumin and oil. Heat the oil for deep-frying in a wok or deep-fryer, then coat the lamb with the cornflour, and deep-fry until crisp. Set aside.

2 Blanch the cabbage in boiling water for 2 minutes, and set aside. In a clean wok, heat the 30ml/2 tbsp oil and fry the ginger and caraway seeds for 1 minute. Add the yellow bean sauce and the sugar, and stir-fry for 30 seconds.

3 Add the lamb and cabbage, and stir for 1 minute. Add 200ml/7fl oz/scant 1 cup water and bring to the boil. Simmer for 5 minutes, then add the tomatoes. Cook until the tomatoes are just soft, then serve hot.

Variation Caraway seeds have a distinctive liquorice flavour and can be overpowering if over-used. Ground cloves makes a good substitute, if you prefer.

Serves 4

300g/11oz lean lamb
5ml/1 tsp ground cumin
15m/1 tbsp vegetable oil
15ml/1 tbsp cornflour (cornstarch)
vegetable oil, for deep-frying
175g/6oz Chinese cabbage,
  sliced into strips
30ml/2 tbsp vegetable oil
15ml/1 tbsp ground ginger
2.5ml/½ tsp caraway seeds,
  finely ground
15ml/1 tbsp yellow bean sauce
15ml/1 tbsp sugar
2 large tomatoes, quartered

Per portion Energy 337kcal/1401kJ; Protein 17g; Carbohydrate 12g, of which sugars 8g; Fat 25g, of which saturates 5g; Cholesterol 56mg; Calcium 51mg; Fibre 1g; Sodium 162mg.

Serves 4

400g/14oz lean mutton or lamb
vegetable oil, for deep-frying
130g/4½oz potatoes, cut into
  bitesize pieces
5ml/1 tsp sugar
30ml/2 tbsp soy sauce
15ml/1 tbsp vegetable oil
25g/1oz grated fresh root ginger
2 garlic cloves, crushed
2.5ml/½ tsp ground Sichuan
  peppercorns
a pinch of Chinese five-spice powder
4 spring onions (scallions),
  cut into 5cm/2in lengths
1 meat stock (bouillon) cube
130g/4½oz carrots, cut into
  bitesize pieces

Tung-Po mutton

Su Tung-Po was a famous poet and gourmet of the Song Dynasty who lived in Hangzhou. This dish, which is attributed to him, has crossed many borders. Muslims from Shandong tweaked the original pork dish to suit their tastes, eschewing pork and alcohol, both of which are forbidden by Islam edict. They also bulk it up with potatoes and carrots to make a substantial winter dish. Curiously, the mutton version seems to have become more mainstream than the pork in many restaurants. In northern China, goat meat would be used for this dish.

1 Cut the mutton or lamb into 2.5cm/1in cubes. Heat the oil for deep-frying in a wok or deep-fryer, and deep-fry the mutton or lamb for 4 minutes. Set aside. Deep-fry the potatoes for 4 minutes, then drain.

2 Transfer the mutton or lamb to a deep pan and add all the remaining ingredients except the potatoes and carrots. Add 1.2 litres/2 pints/5 cups water. Bring to the boil, and simmer for 50 minutes. Add the potatoes and carrots, then cook for a further 10 minutes, until the meat and vegetables are tender.

Variation You can give a lift to the dish by adding 30ml/2 tbsp Shaoxing wine or dry sherry in the last 5 minutes of cooking time, if you like.

Per portion Energy 312kcal/1299kJ; Protein 22g; Carbohydrate 12g, of which sugars 5g; Fat 20g, of which saturates 5g; Cholesterol 74mg; Calcium 39mg; Fibre 2g; Sodium 806mg.

Oxtail stew

When oxtail is cooked in northern China, it tends to be in a thick soup or casserole, sometimes with the addition of herbs like wolf or boxthorn berries for their nutritive properties. Whether you serve it as a soup or a thick stew depends on the amount of water you add, so add more or less water depending on preference. The dish is most welcome as a winter warmer in Beijing, where it can get bitterly cold.

1 Blanch the oxtail pieces in the boiling water for 3 minutes, then drain. This will remove some of the fattiness.

2 Heat the oil in a wok, add the ginger, and stir-fry for 2 minutes. Add the oxtail pieces, and stir-fry for 2 minutes, or until well coated. Add the quartered onion, wine or sherry, oyster sauce, salt, pepper, 1.2 litres/2 pints/5 cups water and the stock cube, then transfer to a deep pan.

3 Bring to the boil and simmer, covered, for 1½ hours or until tender. Top it up with hot water, if necessary. If the dish is intended to be soupy, allow about 200ml/7fl oz/scant 1 cup of liquid per serving with the pieces of the oxtail. Otherwise, serve as a stew by boiling the liquid to reduce the stock.

Serves 4

900g/2lb trimmed oxtail pieces
1.2 litres/2 pints/5 cups boiling water
15ml/1 tbsp vegetable oil
25g/1oz fresh root ginger, sliced
150g/5oz onions, quartered
120ml/4fl oz/½ cup Shaoxing wine
  or dry sherry
30ml/2 tbsp oyster sauce
5ml/1 tsp salt
2.5ml/½ tsp ground black pepper
1 beef stock (bouillon) cube

Cook's tip This dish is suitable for cooking in a pressure cooker. You will need half the quantity of water and it will cook in 1 hour.

Per portion Energy 462kcal/1928kJ; Protein 46g; Carbohydrate 2g, of which sugars 1g; Fat 27g, of which saturates 10g; Cholesterol 169mg; Calcium 26mg; Fibre 0g; Sodium 1309mg.

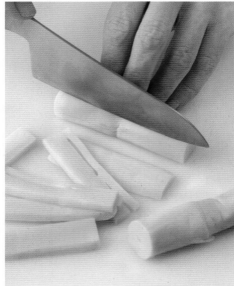

Sliced beef and bamboo shoots

Beef and bamboo shoots have an affinity that is utilised in many dishes, particularly in northern China. In Henan, this dish has pride of place for special occasions and festive days, perhaps because beef is quite expensive, whereas lamb or mutton are the meats that are served every day. When beef is to be stir-fried, it benefits from a little tenderizing, either by being beaten with a mallet or by using a little bicarbonate of soda.

1 Cut the beef across the grain into thin slices about 6cm/2½in long. Tenderize them with a meat mallet on both sides until the slices are extremely thin. Alternatively, mix the beef slices with the bicarbonate of soda.

2 Put the soy sauce, pepper, and wine or sherry in a shallow bowl, add the beef, mix to coat it well, then leave it to marinate for 15 minutes.

3 Slice the bamboo shoots into pieces the same size as the beef, then rinse and drain. Heat the oil in a wok, add the garlic and ginger, and stir-fry for 2 minutes.

4 Add the beef and its marinade, and stir-fry over high heat for 2 minutes. Add the bamboo shoots, yellow bean sauce and sugar, then stir-fry for 1 minute.

5 Blend the cornflour with 120ml/4fl oz/½ cup water and add to the pan. Cook, stirring, for 2 minutes, or until the sauce is thickened. Serve hot, garnished with shredded spring onion.

Cook's tip If you use bicarbonate of soda (baking soda), even tough cuts of beef, such as stewing steak, will be tender enough for stir-frying.

Serves 4

350g/12oz rump (round) or
  sirloin steak
5ml/1 tsp bicarbonate of soda
  (baking soda) (optional)
15ml/1 tbsp dark soy sauce
5ml/1 tsp ground black pepper
15ml/1 tbsp strong Chinese wine,
  such as kaoliang, or dry sherry
175g/6oz bamboo shoots
30ml/2 tbsp vegetable oil
2 garlic cloves, crushed
25g/1oz fresh root ginger,
  peeled and shredded
30ml/2 tbsp yellow bean sauce
5ml/1 tsp sugar
10ml/2 tsp cornflour (cornstarch)
shredded spring onion (scallion),
  to garnish

Per portion Energy 253kcal/1056kJ; Protein 21g; Carbohydrate 7g, of which sugars 3g; Fat 11g, of which saturates 2g; Cholesterol 52mg; Calcium 21mg; Fibre 2g; Sodium 805mg.

Stir-fried venison

Game meats are not commonly cooked outside the northern and western regions of China, as they are not widely available. (This is with the exception of places like Yunnan, where deer are plentiful, and Hong Kong, where a sophisticated clientele expect restaurants to source exotic ingredients for their pleasure.) In Hebei, venison is served as an occasional treat. It is regarded as a 'yang' meat within the yin-yang tenet, meaning that its 'hot' properties will counteract the 'cold' qi energy. When it is tenderized properly, venison is as tasty as beef and is less fatty.

1 Slice the venison thinly and mix with the bicarbonate of soda and wine or sherry. Set aside for at least 3 hours, or preferably overnight.

2 Heat the oil in a wok, add the garlic and stir-fry for 2 minutes. Add the venison and stir-fry over a high heat for 2 minutes, then add the soy sauce, oyster sauce and pepper. Stir-fry for 1 minute more.

3 Slice each mushroom in half, add to the wok and stir-fry for 1 minute. Blend the cornflour with 120ml/4fl oz/½ cup water, then add to the wok. Stir over high heat until the sauce thickens. Serve hot, garnished with sesame seeds and accompanied by noodles.

Serves 4

350g/12oz venison
5ml/1 tsp bicarbonate of soda
 (baking soda)
15ml/1 tbsp Shaoxing wine or
 dry sherry
30ml/2 tbsp vegetable oil
2 garlic cloves, crushed
15ml/1 tbsp dark soy sauce
15ml/1 tbsp oyster sauce
2.5ml/½ tsp ground black pepper
8 Chinese mushrooms, soaked until
 soft, or canned mushrooms
5ml/1 tsp cornflour (cornstarch)
15ml/1 tbsp sesame seeds,
 to garnish
noodles, to serve

Cook's tip Marinating the venison with the wine and bicarbonate of soda (baking soda) overnight will produce the best taste and texture.

Per portion Energy 220kcal/918kJ; Protein 22g; Carbohydrate 8g, of which sugars 0g; Fat 11g, of which saturates 2g; Cholesterol 44mg; Calcium 34mg; Fibre 0g; Sodium 766mg.

Serves 4

450g/1lb pig's liver
2.5ml/½ tsp Chinese
  five-spice powder
30ml/2 tbsp crushed garlic
30ml/2 tbsp rice wine
15ml/1 tbsp vegetable oil
30ml/2 tbsp fresh root ginger,
  peeled and cut into thin strips
15ml/1 tbsp oyster sauce
30ml/2 tbsp dark soy sauce
2.5ml/½ tsp ground black pepper
30ml/2 tbsp sesame oil
5ml/1 tsp cornflour (cornstarch)
3 spring onions (scallions), cut into
  5cm/2in pieces

Cook's tip It is easier to slice the liver thinly if you place it in the freezer until it firms up.

Per portion Energy 223kcal/934kJ; Protein 25g; Carbohydrate 4g, of which sugars 1g; Fat 11g, of which saturates 2g; Cholesterol 293mg; Calcium 22mg; Fibre 0g; Sodium 681mg.

Liver in five spices

It can be quite difficult to cook liver to perfection. It demands careful cooking because it toughens up when overcooked by even a few minutes. There are also variable textures in each liver: some become chewy, whereas others cook to a delectable tenderness. It is thought that the age of the animal has a lot to do with this, but you never can tell how each liver will react to cooking; it is always best to avoid over-cooking it.

1 Slice the liver thinly (*see* Cook's Tip). Mix the Chinese five-spice powder, garlic and rice wine in a bowl, then add the liver. Mix well, then leave to marinate for 25 minutes.

2 Heat the oil in a wok, add the ginger, and stir-fry until crisp and golden brown. Add the liver and its marinade, the oyster sauce, soy sauce, pepper and sesame oil, and cook, stirring, for 2 minutes.

3 Blend 105ml/7 tbsp water with the cornflour and add to the wok. Cook, stirring, until the sauce thickens and the liver is cooked through. Add the spring onions during the last 30 seconds and stir to mix well. Serve hot.

Shredded kidneys in wine sauce

The kidneys in this dish are cut in such a way that each piece becomes a frill, although it is described in the recipe name as 'shredded'. The recipe is a close cousin of Liver in Five Spices, and the two dishes are often cooked at the same time, making a robust pair of dishes with restorative properties. Kidneys are believed to regulate urinary functions – in traditional Chinese herbal medicine, like relates to like. Kidneys tend to be an acquired taste because they do have a strong ammonia smell and flavour. To reduce this, make sure every bit of the white membrane is removed and that the kidneys are soaked in cold water for an hour or so before cooking.

1 Slice each kidney in half. With a sharp knife, remove all the white membrane and core. Cut each kidney half into four pieces. Holding each piece firmly at one end, make slices about 1cm/½in away from your fingers, right through the kidney and tapering at each end. This makes a frill on each piece. Soak the pieces in cold water for at least 15 minutes.

2 Mix the wine or sherry and garlic in a shallow bowl, add the kidney pieces, mix well and leave to marinate for 1 hour.

3 Heat the oil in a wok, add the spring onions and stir-fry for 1 minute. Add the ginger, Chinese five-spice powder and dark soy sauce. Stir-fry for 1 minute, then add 120ml/ 4fl oz/½ cup water and bring to the boil.

4 Add the kidney pieces and cook over medium heat until cooked through. Garnish with fresh coriander and shredded spring onion, and serve.

Serves 4

2 pig's kidneys
30ml/2 tbsp Shaoxing wine
  or dry sherry
3 garlic cloves, crushed
30ml/2 tbsp vegetable oil
3 spring onions (scallions),
  cut into 5cm/2in pieces
4 slices pickled ginger,
  sliced into strips
a pinch of Chinese
  five-spice powder
15ml/1 tbsp dark soy sauce
fresh coriander (cilantro) and
  shredded spring onion (scallion),
  to garnish

Per portion Energy 159kcal/664kJ; Protein 14g; Carbohydrate 2g, of which sugars 1g; Fat 10g, of which saturates 2g; Cholesterol 359mg; Calcium 21mg; Fibre 0g; Sodium 391mg.

Four treasures meat

Numerology can have different meanings from one region to the next. It tends to be a dialectic thing: the number four is avoided at all costs in Guangzhou, as in Cantonese it is phonetically the same as the word 'death'. In Mandarin and other regional dialects, the number four does not have any negative symbolism, and the Four Treasures Meat dish is popular in Beijing. Traditionally, the 'four treasures' refer to poultry webs, wings, tongues and viscera – a mixture that would not go down well with conservative diners! Here, I have taken a modern approach and used alternatives that taste excellent together.

1 Remove the skin from the duck breast and slice into 1cm/½in wide pieces. Remove the skin from the belly pork and slice as for the duck. Heat the oil for deep-frying in a wok or deep-fryer, and deep-fry the duck and belly pork pieces for 3 minutes (in batches, if necessary), then drain on kitchen paper, and set aside.

2 Wash and drain the chicken livers, then cut the larger pieces into two. Slice through the pig's kidney, and cut out the white core and membrane. Cut into 4cm/1½in pieces and make surface criss-cross cuts in each. (When they are cooked, each piece will open up like a flower.)

3 Heat the 15ml/1 tbsp oil in a clean wok, add the spring onions and ginger, and stir-fry for 2 minutes. Add duck, pork, livers and kidney, and stir-fry for 2 minutes.

4 Add the soy sauce, yellow bean sauce, rice wine, sugar and pepper, and cook, stirring, for 1 minute. Add 200ml/7fl oz/scant 1 cup water, bring to the boil, and simmer for 5 minutes.

5 Blend the tapioca with a little water and add to the wok. Stir until the sauce thickens, and serve hot, garnished with sliced spring onion.

Serves 4

150g/5oz duck breast
150g/5oz belly pork
vegetable oil, for deep-frying
115g/4oz chicken livers
1 pig's kidney
15ml/1 tbsp vegetable oil
2 spring onions (scallions), chopped
25g/1oz fresh root ginger, grated
30ml/2 tbsp dark soy sauce
15ml/1 tbsp yellow bean sauce
15ml/1 tbsp rice wine
2.5ml/½ tsp sugar
2.5ml/½ tsp ground black pepper
5ml/1 tsp tapioca flour
sliced spring onion (scallion),
  to garnish

Cook's tip You can choose four kinds of any other meat, fish, shellfish or vegetable for this stir-fry.

Per portion Energy 288kcal/1202kJ; Protein 25g; Carbohydrate 3g, of which sugars 2g; Fat 19g, of which saturates 5g; Cholesterol 305mg; Calcium 24mg; Fibre 1g; Sodium 247mg.

Pancakes, bread and noodles

The staple grain in the north is wheat, and it is transformed into myriad products. Where as rice is central to meals elsewhere in China, steamed breads take its place in those provinces where no rice can be grown. Wheat-based noodles, sometimes enriched with egg, are also traditionally popular. They become all-in-one meals, especially when tossed with fish, shellfish or meat.

Starchy fillers and festival treats

Since the climate of the northern provinces is not suited to growing rice, the grain (ubiquitous in the rest of China) has never formed part of the local menus. Today it is enjoyed here as it is in the rest of the world, but the local favourites remain breads and noodles.

Apart from the famous Mandarin Pancakes, which are traditionally served with Peking Duck, very few pancakes are offered plain; they are usually filled with a meat-based or sweet mixture. Bean paste is a common filler, and can be either savoury or sweet.

Steamed breads tend to form the carbohydrate staple in the northern provinces, no matter what else is on the table. They are made from low-gluten wheat flour, which is available in Chinese stores.

During festive occasions, noodles are prepared with great pride, and families sit down to delicious offerings, often with eels, minced beef or lamb. Throughout China, noodles have always been regarded as symbolic of longevity, though many modernists today regard this with only bemusement. Nevertheless, it is still traditional for noodles to make a grand appearance at every special event.

In Beijing, hand-pulled noodles are especially famous, and they are on sale every day from street-food stalls. They are to northern China what pasta is to Italy, and the cooking of noodles has not changed greatly for centuries. Many dishes have become iconic in Chinese restaurants around the world, and there does not seem to be a limit to the dishes chefs can create with noodles.

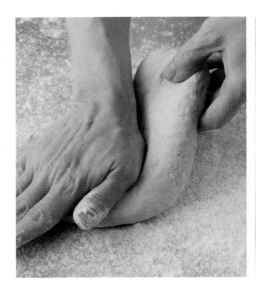

Mandarin pancakes

Peking duck would not be the same without these pancakes. I learned how to make them many moons ago from the master of Chinese cuisine, the late, venerable Kenneth Lo, when I was teaching at his culinary institute in London. They are extremely easy to make, requiring no special skill, but a lot of patience. Of course, the easy option is to buy them ready-made, but think how impressed your guests will be when you next entertain and serve your own Peking duck, accompanied by your own pancakes!

Makes about 12

200g/7oz plain/scant 2 cups
  (all-purpose) flour
150ml/¼ pint/⅔ cup boiling water
15ml/1 tbsp vegetable oil
Peking Duck, to serve (*see* recipe
  page 84)

Cook's tips
• Any unused pancakes can be wrapped and frozen or chilled for up to 5 days.
• When using them from frozen, always steam them rather than frying or heating them in the microwave.

1 Sift the flour into a large heatproof bowl, and gradually pour in the boiling water, stirring with a pair of chopsticks or a wooden spoon. Do not add any more water, even if the dough appears rather dry. Set aside to cool.

2 Turn out the dough on to a floured work surface and knead for 10 minutes, or until it is firm and slightly elastic. Set aside for 30 minutes to rest.

3 Roll out the dough into a long sausage about 2.5cm/1in in diameter. Slice into 12 pieces and roll each one into a small ball.

4 Flatten each ball with the palm of your hand and roll out into a paper-thin circle, about 13cm/5in in diameter. Repeat with the remaining balls of dough.

5 Brush each pancake with oil on one side and pair them up, one on top of another, oiled sides facing together. Heat a frying pan with a little oil and fry each double pancake for 1 minute, or until brown bubbles begin to appear. Flip over and cook the other side for 1 minute.

6 Gently peel the pancakes apart. Fold each in half and stack them on a large plate that will fit inside your steamer. Steam for 25 minutes, then serve with Peking duck.

Per portion Energy 68kcal/288kJ; Protein 2g; Carbohydrate 13g, of which sugars 0g; Fat 1g, of which saturates 0g; Cholesterol 0mg; Calcium 23mg; Fibre 1g; Sodium 1mg.

Bean paste cakes

The bean paste here is not the sweet variety made from red beans, but a paste made from shelled mung beans, which is cooked as a savoury filling. These beans are sold already shelled, but they do have to be soaked overnight. The dish is not known in most of China, coming as it does from Tianjin, a large municipality that borders Beijing. I was introduced to this savoury cake by my neighbours from Liaoning and found it most unusual, with its blend of crispy bacon and soft mung bean paste.

1 To make the filling, boil the mung beans in 300ml/½ pint/1¼ cups water for 15 minutes. Drain in a colander until nearly dry, then transfer to a mixing bowl, and mash with a potato masher to make a smooth paste.

2 Heat a wok and fry the pork or bacon fat for 2 minutes, then add the spring onions. Stir-fry for 1 minute, then add the soy sauce, pepper and sesame oil. Cook, stirring, for a further 1 minute, then transfer to a large bowl.

3 Add the mashed mung beans, and stir well. Set aside while you make the batter.

4 Sift the flour and cornflour into a mixing bowl and add the salt. Stir to mix, and then gradually add the boiling water, stirring well. Stir in 15ml/1 tbsp oil. Allow to cool, then transfer to a floured work surface, and knead for 5 minutes.

5 Roll out the dough into a long sausage shape and cut into four pieces. Flatten each piece into a thin round about 3mm/⅛in thick. Divide the mung bean mixture between the rounds – there should be about 15ml/1 tbsp on each. Fold and draw the sides into the centre. Twist and pinch off any excess. Seal with a dab of water and shape into a round, flat cake.

6 Place the cakes on a lightly oiled plate that will fit into your steamer, and steam for 10 minutes. Remove and allow to cool.

7 Heat a frying pan with the remaining oil, and cook the cakes, sealed side down, until golden brown, then flip them over to fry the other side. You will need to do this in batches. When brown and crispy, remove and drain on kitchen paper. Serve with a chilli sauce dip.

Makes about 4 large cakes

150g/5oz/1¼ cups plain
 (all-purpose) flour
15ml/1 tbsp cornflour (cornstarch)
a pinch of salt
120ml/4fl oz/½ cup boiling water
90ml/6 tbsp vegetable oil
chilli sauce dip, to serve

For the filling
90g/3½oz shelled mung beans,
 soaked overnight (*see* Cook's Tip)
75g/3oz pork fat or bacon fat,
 finely chopped
2 spring onions (scallions),
 finely chopped
15ml/1 tbsp light soy sauce
2.5ml/½ tsp ground black pepper
30ml/2 tbsp sesame oil

Cook's tip When soaking the beans overnight, use enough water to just cover the beans. By the next day, all the water will have been absorbed.

Per portion Energy 356kcal/1485kJ; Protein 6g; Carbohydrate 34g, of which sugars 1g; Fat 22g, of which saturates 5g; Cholesterol 13mg; Calcium 68mg; Fibre 3g; Sodium 291mg.

Steamed bread

Made from wheat flour, steamed breads account for much of the staple carbohydrates eaten in northern China. This popular bread, called man tou, is believed to have originated here during the Song Dynasty (960–1279). The cooks of Sichuan refute this, however, claiming it was their invention. Until food distribution became more efficient in modern China, rice was not integral to northern meals; steamed breads were the staple of choice. Today, steamed breads are still central to many northern meals.

1 Mix the sugar with the yeast in a small bowl and add 100ml/3½fl oz/scant ½ cup lukewarm water. Put into a warm place. After about 15 minutes it will begin to froth.

2 Put the flour into a large bowl and make a well in the centre. Pour in the yeast mixture and mix well. Add more lukewarm water, a little at a time, up to about 200ml/7fl oz/scant 1 cup. Add just enough to make a pliable dough.

3 Transfer the dough to a well-floured work surface and knead vigorously for 10 minutes, or until the dough is elastic and smooth. Put into a lightly oiled bowl, cover with a damp dish towel and leave in a warm place to rise for 1 hour, or until doubled in bulk.

4 Knock back (punch down) the dough to its original size, then leave for a further 30 minutes to rise again.

5 Knead on a floured work surface for another 15 minutes before shaping. There are many ways you can shape man tou. The most basic is to roll the dough into a sausage, then press it into a flat rectangle about 5mm/¼in thick. Lift up the long side and roll it up tightly like a Swiss roll (jelly roll). Press the end to seal, and slice into 2cm/¾in rounds.

6 Grease a plate that will fit into your steamer with the fat or oil. Place the dough rounds on the plate, and steam them for 10 minutes, or until they have puffed up. You may need to do this in batches, depending on the size of your steamer. Serve with any braised or roasted meat dish.

Makes about 20

15ml/1 tbsp sugar
15ml/1 tbsp active dried yeast
450g/1lb/4 cups low-gluten wheat flour, plus extra for dusting
lard, white cooking fat or vegetable oil, for greasing

Cook's tips
• Any unused rolls can be chilled, covered and re-steamed for 5 minutes for serving.
• You can also use 1 sachet (7g/¼oz) of easy bake (rapid-rise) dried yeast; omit the sugar and frothing step and add it with the flour.

Per portion Energy 77kcal/326kJ; Protein 2g; Carbohydrate 17g, of which sugars 0g; Fat 0g, of which saturates 0g; Cholesterol 0mg; Calcium 32mg; Fibre 1g; Sodium 1mg.

Serves 4

400g/14oz fresh yellow egg noodles
200g/7oz eel cutlets
5ml/1 tsp ground black pepper
30ml/2 tbsp sesame oil
30ml/2 tbsp Shaoxing wine
  or dry sherry
30ml/2 tbsp vegetable oil
15ml/1 tbsp crushed garlic
2 spring onions (scallions), cut into
  2.5cm/1in strips
90g/3½oz beansprouts
30ml/2 tbsp oyster sauce

Beijing eel noodles

If you have a fondness for eels, you will love this sumptuous dish. As a fish with scarcely any bones, eel is undeservedly maligned and often passed over. Eel flesh is smooth and firm, and is excellent cooked in a rich wine sauce. Noodles work well with its richness, and beansprouts and celery give the requisite crunch. Get your fishmonger to cut each eel into chunks, so it will be easier to slice them into strips.

1 Blanch the noodles in boiling water, and drain. Cut the eel into strips. Mix the pepper, sesame oil, and wine or sherry in a bowl, add the eel strips, and leave to marinate for 15 minutes.

2 Heat the oil in a wok, add the garlic, and stir-fry until golden brown. Add the spring onions and stir-fry for 1 minute.

3 Add the eels and their marinade, and cook, stirring, over high heat for 2 minutes. Remove the eels from the wok using a slotted spoon, and set aside.

4 Add the noodles and beansprouts to the wok and stir-fry for 2 minutes. Add 200ml/7fl oz/ scant 1 cup water, the oyster sauce and eels, and cook, stirring, for 3 minutes, until the eels are cooked through. Serve immediately.

Per portion Energy 637kcal/2674kJ; Protein 22g; Carbohydrate 75g, of which sugars 3g; Fat 29g, of which saturates 6g; Cholesterol 105mg; Calcium 53mg; Fibre 6g; Sodium 539mg.

Minced lamb noodles

In the province of Liaoning, minced lamb takes the place of minced pork in many dishes, with noodles being the favourite accompaniment. The province, together with Jilin and Heilongjiang, as well as a part of Inner Mongolia, is within the region that was formerly known as Manchuria. Liaoning cuisine is heavily influenced by that of the Manchus, as well as that of Beijing. As a result, much of its cooking is refined and elegant. Today, Liaoning is known for producing gourmet chefs, and scarcely a week passes without some cooking competition taking place.

1 In a mixing bowl, mix the minced lamb with the wine or sherry, sesame oil, cornflour and salt, then set aside for 15 minutes.

2 Heat the oil in a wok, add the garlic and stir-fry for 2 minutes. Add the minced lamb and its marinade, and stir-fry for 2 minutes. Add 200ml/7fl oz/scant 1 cup water and the dark soy sauce, and cook, stirring, for a further 2 minutes.

3 Add the noodles, spring onions and pepper, and cook, stirring, for 3 minutes more, or until the noodles and lamb are well mixed, the lamb is cooked through, and the spring onions are soft and succulent.

Cook's tip Minced (ground) pork or beef can be cooked in the same way, with very little difference in cooking time. Marinating the meat in wine also helps to tenderize it.

Serves 4

175g/6oz/1½ cups lean minced
  (ground) lamb
30ml/2 tbsp Shaoxing wine
  or dry sherry
15ml/1 tbsp sesame oil
5ml/1 tsp cornflour (cornstarch)
2.5ml/½ tsp salt
15ml/1 tbsp vegetable oil
3 garlic cloves, crushed
15ml/1 tbsp dark soy sauce
200g/7oz fresh wheat or egg noodles
4 spring onions (scallions), cut into
  5cm/2in pieces
2.5ml/½ tsp ground black pepper

Per portion Energy 351kcal/1470kJ; Protein 16g; Carbohydrate 39g, of which sugars 2g; Fat 15g, of which saturates 4g; Cholesterol 47mg; Calcium 36mg; Fibre 3g; Sodium 584mg.

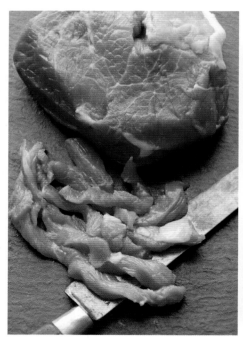

Stir-fried noodles and lamb

Lamb is by far the most popular meat in the north, and Muslim chefs from Shanxi are particularly skilled at cooking even the toughest cuts. This dish is reputed to have been invented by the first of the Manchurian emperors of the Qing Dynasty. While they reigned, the arts flourished and the Mandarinate was filled with educated people, gourmets and cultured officials. Because this is a Muslim dish, rice vinegar is used instead of wine.

1 Cut the lamb into thin strips. Heat the oil in a wok, add the garlic and ginger, and stir-fry for 2 minutes. Add the lamb and stir-fry for 2 minutes.

2 Add 200ml/7fl oz/scant 1 cup water, bring to the boil, and simmer for 5 minutes, until the lamb is cooked through. Remove the lamb with a slotted spoon, and set aside.

3 In the same wok, add the rice vinegar, sesame oil, soy sauce and leek slices, and cook, stirring, for 2 minutes, or until the leek is soft.

4 Add the noodles and pepper, and continue to stir until well mixed. The sauce should be just thick enough to coat the noodles.

5 Return the lamb to the wok and heat through, stirring as little as possible, so that you can then serve the dish with the lamb heaped on top of the noodles.

Cook's tip You can also use a tougher cut of lamb or mutton. If so, mix it with 5ml/1 tsp bicarbonate of soda (baking soda) before cooking to tenderize it.

Serves 4

175g/6oz lean lamb
15ml/1 tbsp vegetable oil
2 garlic cloves, crushed
25g/1oz fresh root ginger, peeled and shredded
15ml/1 tbsp rice vinegar
15ml/1 tbsp sesame oil
15ml/1 tbsp dark soy sauce
1 leek, thinly sliced
200g/7oz fresh wheat or egg noodles
2.5ml/½ tsp ground black pepper

Per portion Energy 342kcal/1434kJ; Protein 16g; Carbohydrate 38g, of which sugars 2g; Fat 15g, of which saturates 4g; Cholesterol 47mg; Calcium 28mg; Fibre 3g; Sodium 337mg.

Noodles with minced beef

Although not as famous as Sichuan's dan dan noodles, Shanxi takes pride in the glorious minced beef noodles that appear on local menus. Noodles are taken very seriously in the north of China – as much as rice is in the south of the country – and there are many styles of cooking wheat, rice or mung-bean noodles. When noodles constitute the main dish in family meals, there are very few, if any, other dishes. This recipe makes a one-dish meal that contains all the nutritional constituents: starch, protein and vegetables. With large families living on a tight budget, this is a sure way to ensure that everyone can receive a sustaining, nutritious meal.

1 Blanch or cook the noodles according to the packet instructions. Drain and set aside.

2 Heat the oil in a wok and fry the garlic for 2 minutes, then add the minced beef and fry for 2 minutes. Add the oyster sauce, sesame oil, dark soy sauce, Chinese cabbage and pepper, and fry for 2 minutes.

3 Mix the cornflour with 90ml/6 tbsp water and add to the wok. Stir until the sauce is thick. Add the noodles and continue to stir until the noodles, beef and vegetables are well mixed. Serve, garnished with chopped spring onions.

Cook's tip Stir-fried noodles are usually cooked with just enough liquid to make a fairly thick sauce. If you prefer noodles that are more moist, increase the amount of water, and adjust with a little more soy sauce to taste.

Serves 4

200g/7oz dried wheat noodles
15ml/1 tbsp vegetable oil
2 garlic cloves, crushed
150g/5oz/generous 1 cup minced (ground) beef
30ml/2 tbsp oyster sauce
15ml/1 tbsp sesame oil
15ml/1 tbsp dark soy sauce
90g/3½oz Chinese cabbage, thinly sliced
2.5ml/½ tsp ground black pepper
15ml/1 tbsp cornflour (cornstarch)
2 spring onions (scallions), chopped, to garnish

Per portion Energy 342kcal/1439kJ; Protein 15g; Carbohydrate 44g, of which sugars 2g; Fat 13g, of which saturates 2g; Cholesterol 44mg; Calcium 36mg; Fibre 3g; Sodium 556mg.

Vegetables, nuts, eggs and tofu

Since much of north China is remote and climatically harsh, it does not enjoy the green cornucopia with which some of the other regions are blessed. Nonetheless, locals are adept at coaxing the best of any vegetables derived from their humble plots. The art of drying and pickling excess greens has been their saviour for centuries, and these preserved vegetables are then on hand to add an extra dimension to family meals during lean times.

Crisp, crunchy, fresh and healthy

As in the rest of China, the tenet of yin-yang (or universal balance) comes into play whenever vegetables are prepared. The symbiosis of textures, flavours and colours underscores the essence of vegetable dishes, whether served as a vegetarian meal or something to accompany meat, poultry, fish or shellfish. Humble though they may be, vegetables such as beansprouts, bamboo shoots, cabbage, pak choi (bok choy), aubergines (eggplants) and mushrooms are combined and prepared in such skilful ways, that they can often overshadow the grandest meat and poultry dishes.

Peanuts are grown in the northern provinces, and they are seen as much more than a crunchy snack. They can be used in many recipes, and they are seasoned and boiled to make tasty nibbles.

Eggs also feature in this chapter, a favourite ingredient of thrifty cooks, who can use them to whip up nutritious meals when fresh vegetables are scarce. They are combined with tofu and preserved vegetables in the Steamed Egg Custard recipe from Hebei.

Tofu is one of China's favourite ingredients, and it is put to good use in the northern provinces. Being relatively inexpensive and very nutritious, it is a popular food for vegetarians and meat-eaters alike. During Taoist and Buddhist festivals, tofu is especially popular. Along with vegetables like beans, aubergines and leafy greens, it takes centre stage in stews and stir-fries. In China, vegetable dishes are not reserved for vegetarians; they simply make good eating.

Pickled Chinese cabbage

Chinese cabbage – also known as napa cabbage – is a large, leafy vegetable with firm, white stalks and pale leaves that are similar to cos or romaine lettuce in texture. It is generally cooked, but is also fantastic pickled, to be served as an accompaniment to roast meats and poultry. Do not wash the cabbage before pickling it, as any moisture can harbour bacteria and ruin the pickle. Separate each large stalk and wipe clean with a dry cloth or kitchen paper to remove any traces of soil near the root end. This pickle is typical of Jilin cooking. It has a very crisp texture and a tangy, clean taste. Make this 2 days before you need it.

1 Cut the cabbage into 1cm/½in wide strips and shred the leaves into small pieces. Place the stalks and leaves into a large bowl and sprinkle the salt all over. Toss well, then cover and leave overnight.

2 By the next day the cabbage will have softened. Take out a handful at a time and squeeze out any moisture. Pat dry with kitchen paper.

3 Place the vinegar in a pan and bring to the boil. Add the cabbage and simmer for 2 minutes, working in batches, if necessary. Remove using a slotted spoon and drain in a colander. Leave the vinegar on the heat.

4 Remove the stalks from the chillies, and slice each chilli in half lengthways. Discard the seeds. Add the chillies to the boiling vinegar, and cook for 1 minute, then drain in a colander.

5 Mix the cabbage and chillies together, add the sugar and toss well. Cover and set aside overnight, then stir well to serve as a side pickle.

Serves 6–8

1 large Chinese cabbage
15ml/1 tbsp salt
475ml/16fl oz/2 cups white vinegar
3 fresh red chillies
5ml/1 tsp sugar

Variation For an even spicier pickle, much like Korean kimchi, add 30ml/2 tbsp chilli paste to the blanched pak choi and steep for 2 days before serving.

Per portion Energy 20kcal/80kJ; Protein 1g; Carbohydrate 2g, of which sugars 2g; Fat 0g, of which saturates 0g; Cholesterol 0mg; Calcium 16mg; Fibre 1g; Sodium 251mg.

Serves 4

450g/1lb raw peanuts
5ml/1 tsp Sichuan peppercorns
1 small cinnamon stick
a pinch of ground cloves
2 star anise
25g/1oz fresh root ginger, grated
5ml/1 tsp sugar

Cook's tip If you do not have any muslin (cheesecloth), the spices can be added directly to the water. You will need to drain the nuts carefully to make sure the spices are all removed.

Boiled peanuts

Peanuts are not considered merely a crunchy snack in most of China. In northern provinces, they take starring roles, possibly because there is some symbolism attached to them: the Chinese word for peanuts, hua shen, is a synonym for 'success'. They are boiled, fried and roasted, as well as processed into oil. Buy them raw, with their skins on, and they can be cooked in a seasoned broth. Serve with cold dishes, or as nibbles.

1 Place the peanuts in a pan of water, bring to the boil, and simmer for 30 minutes. Allow to cool, then drain. Take handfuls of the nuts and rub them together gently to remove the skins. Rinse and drain.

2 Bring 1.2 litres/2 pints/5 cups water to the boil, and add the nuts. Place the Sichuan peppercorns, cinnamon stick, ground cloves, star anise and ginger in a piece of muslin (cheesecloth), and tie it together with cook's string. Place in the pan with the peanuts.

3 Simmer for 45 minutes, then remove the spices, and drain the peanuts. Leave to cool before serving.

Per portion Energy 641kcal/2663kJ; Protein 29g; Carbohydrate 16g, of which sugars 8g; Fat 52g, of which saturates 10g; Cholesterol 0mg; Calcium 69mg; Fibre 8g; Sodium 3mg.

Cold aubergine salad

In the chilly northern provinces cold vegetable dishes or salads are not overly popular, but when summer arrives, these dishes do appear on menus. Even if a vegetable dish is served cold, it is very rarely raw; there is always at least some gentle cooking before assembly. Aubergine is a good choice for this process, as it has a texture and taste that are not diminished when served chilled. This recipe comes from Tianjin.

1 Cut off the aubergine stalks, and slice the aubergines in half lengthways. Slice them horizontally into semi-circles, each 1cm/½in wide. Place the aubergine slices in a colander, sprinkle with salt, and set them aside for 15 minutes.

2 Taking a handful at a time, squeeze out the moisture from the aubergines, and pat them dry with kitchen paper. Place the water in a pan, bring to the boil, add the aubergines, and simmer for 5 minutes. Drain thoroughly.

3 In a bowl, mix the sesame oil with the vinegar and sugar, and stir until the sugar dissolves. Add the boiled aubergine slices, and toss well. Transfer to a serving bowl, and garnish with sesame seeds. Serve at room temperature or chilled, with preserved sweet turnip.

Serves 4

400g/14oz aubergine (eggplant)
2.5ml/½ tsp salt
350ml/12fl oz/1½ cups water
30ml/2 tbsp sesame oil
15ml/1 tbsp rice vinegar
2.5ml/½ tsp sugar
15ml/1 tbsp sesame seeds
5ml/1 tsp preserved sweet
  turnip, chopped

Cook's tip Courgettes (zucchini) can be prepared in the same way.

Per portion Energy 108kcal/446kJ; Protein 2g; Carbohydrate 3g, of which sugars 10g; Fat 2g, of which saturates 2g; Cholesterol 0mg; Calcium 36mg; Fibre 2g; Sodium 249mg.

Steamed egg custard

This is a delicious, light dish that is ideal with congee and is very easy to prepare. It requires only eggs and tofu: two products that have a great affinity with each other. In Hebei province it is a favourite summer dish that provides a perfect contrast to deep-fried meat and chicken dishes. The seasonings and toppings can be varied to taste, but sesame oil and pepper are typical of northern China. Use soft or silken tofu for the best results.

1 Lightly beat the eggs (do not over-beat) and season with pepper, soy sauce and sugar. In a separate bowl, mash the tofu with a fork, add the sesame oil and 45ml/3 tbsp water, then mash again until smooth.

2 Add the egg mixture and chopped spring onion to the tofu, and stir well to incorporate. Transfer to a deep plate or shallow bowl that will fit into your steamer. Sprinkle the chopped winter vegetable over the top, and steam for 10 minutes, or until the custard is set.

Serves 4

4 eggs
2.5ml/½ tsp ground white pepper
15ml/1 tbsp light soy sauce
a pinch of sugar
275g/10oz soft tofu
15ml/1 tbsp sesame oil
1 spring onion (scallion), chopped
5ml/1 tsp chopped preserved winter
   vegetable (tung chai)

Variation If you are not serving this to vegetarians, you can add 30ml/2 tbsp minced (ground) pork or chicken to the egg mixture and mix well. Continue with step 2, but steam for 15 minutes, until the meat is cooked through.

Per portion Energy 177kcal/735kJ; Protein 14g; Carbohydrate 1g, of which sugars 1g; Fat 13g, of which saturates 3g; Cholesterol 232mg; Calcium 391mg; Fibre 0g; Sodium 267mg.

pServes 4

450g/1lb potatoes, peeled
  and cut into 5mm/¼in slices
45ml/3 tbsp vegetable oil
30ml/2 tbsp dark soy sauce
a pinch of Chinese five-spice powder
2.5ml/½ tsp ground
  Sichuan peppercorns
15ml/1 tbsp sesame oil

Variations

• Cut the potatoes into 2cm/¾in dice instead of slices for a more chunky texture, if you like.
• Root vegetables like swede (rutabaga), turnip and sweet potato work very well cooked this way.

Per portion Energy 224kcal/932kJ; Protein 3g; Carbohydrate 20g, of which sugars 1g; Fat 15g, of which saturates 2g; Cholesterol 0mg; Calcium 7mg; Fibre 2g; Sodium 437mg.

Soy sauce potatoes

I was served this unusual Beijing dish at a dinner hosted by a friend who said his grandfather had been a chef in the court of the last emperor, Pu Yi, before the fall of the Qing Dynasty. I was curious about the use of potatoes, as they are not a typical Chinese ingredient, appearing rarely on menus. It it thought the dish was brought to Beijing from Shanghai, which has been a bustling international centre for centuries.

1 Boil the potatoes in plenty of water for 5 minutes, or until just soft. Gently lift out with a slotted spoon to prevent them from breaking up. Place in a colander to drain thoroughly.

2 Heat the oil in a wok until smoking. Working in batches, add the potato slices, and fry until golden. Do not crowd the wok or they will not become brown. Remove each batch and drain on kitchen paper.

3 Remove all but 15ml/1 tbsp oil and add the soy sauce, Chinese five-spice powder, pepper, sesame oil and 45ml/3 tbsp water. Add the potatoes and stir gently, turning them over so that they are thoroughly coated with the sauce. Serve hot.

Serves 4

1 whole green cabbage
15ml/1 tbsp sugar
30ml/2 tbsp rice vinegar
15ml/1 tbsp light soy sauce
5ml/1 tsp cornflour (cornstarch)
3 pickled plums or limes

Sweet-and-sour cabbage

As a rule, sweet-and-sour sauces are usually cooked with meat or seafood, but in Shandong province, local vegetables like green cabbage, pak choi (bok choy) and robust root vegetables often get the sweet-tart treatment. The sweetening agent here is ordinary sugar, which is blended with rice vinegar to create the requisite balance. It also includes some pickled limes or plums for an extra kick of flavour.

1 Cut the cabbage into thin strips, 1cm/½in wide. Bring a pan of water to the boil and blanch the cabbage for 2–3 minutes, until just soft but not mushy. Drain until quite dry.

2 In a pan, mix the sugar with the rice vinegar, 120ml/4fl oz/½ cup water and the soy sauce, and warm over gentle heat until the sugar has dissolved. Turn up the heat, and bring the sauce to the boil. Allow it to simmer for 1–2 minutes.

3 Meanwhile, mix the cornflour with a little water. Add to the sauce and stir until it thickens. Slice the pickled plums or limes into small pieces and add to the sauce.

4 Place the cabbage in a large pan and warm it up a little. Add the sauce and toss well to blend, then heat through without boiling. Serve warm with roasted meats or poultry.

Variation Root vegetables and mustard greens also work well with a sweet-and-sour sauce. Slice and blanch until soft in the same way before mixing with the sauce.

Per portion Energy 36kcal/150kJ; Protein 2g; Carbohydrate 6g, of which sugars 5g; Fat 0g, of which saturates 0g; Cholesterol 0mg; Calcium 47mg; Fibre 3g; Sodium mg.

Fried leeks with hot sauce

In open and wet markets all over Beijing, vegetable vendors sell stacked heaps of leeks, many with damp soil still clinging to the roots, among other local produce. Leeks are a member of the allium family with garlic and onions, and share much the same pungency. In southern China, they are eaten for symbolic reasons: in the Cantonese dialect, the word for 'leeks' rhymes with the word for 'count', so it bodes well for prosperity. In northern China, however, they are popular merely for their delicious taste and texture, both of which are showcased in this dish.

1 Slice the leeks, diagonally, into pieces 2.5cm/1in wide. Wash them in plenty of cold water to remove any soil that often clings to the insides of the white stalks. Drain thoroughly.

2 Heat the oil in a wok and, when smoking, add the leeks. Stir-fry over high heat for 2 minutes. Add the chilli paste, light soy sauce, sugar and wine or sherry, and stir-fry for a further 2 minutes.

3 Mix the cornflour with 60ml/4 tbsp water, and add to the wok. Stir until thickened slightly, then serve hot.

Serves 4

4 leeks, white parts only
30ml/2 tbsp vegetable oil
15ml/1 tbsp chilli paste
15ml/1 tbsp light soy sauce
2.5ml/½ tsp sugar
15ml/1 tbsp Shaoxing wine
  or dry sherry
5ml/1 tsp cornflour (cornstarch)

Cook's tip Wash the green parts of the leeks thoroughly, then use them to make vegetable stock, if you like. Use 100g/3¾oz leeks to 200ml/7fl oz/ scant 1 cup water.

Per portion Energy 98kcal/405kJ; Protein 2g; Carbohydrate 4g, of which sugars 2g; Fat 8g, of which saturates 1g; Cholesterol 0mg; Calcium 20mg; Fibre 2g; Sodium 182mg.

Fried beans in garlic sauce

The beans used here are normal green beans, about 7.5cm/3in long; however, any other type of bean, such as broad (fava) beans, can be cooked in the same way. When blanched as a pre-cooking step, they retain their crunch and green colour. In Hebei, yellow bean sauce is the key seasoning, and it is salty enough that the dish requires no additional salt.

1 Put the garlic in a small bowl with the ginger, pepper, yellow bean sauce, sugar and sesame oil, then mix together.

2 Boil a small pan of water and blanch the beans in it for 2 minutes. Drain.

3 Heat the oil in a wok, add the sauce, and stir-fry for 1 minute. Add the blanched beans, and cook, stirring, over high heat for 2 minutes.

4 Add 100ml/3½fl oz/scant ½ cup water. Continue to cook, stirring, for 1 minute, or until well mixed and aromatic. Serve hot with plain rice or noodles.

Serves 4

4 garlic cloves, crushed
25g/1oz fresh root ginger, grated
1.5ml/¼ tsp ground
  Sichuan peppercorns
15ml/1 tbsp yellow bean sauce
2.5ml/½ tsp sugar
30ml/2 tbsp sesame oil
400g/14oz green beans, trimmed
15ml/1 tbsp vegetable oil
plain boiled rice or noodles, to serve

Variation Replace the yellow bean sauce with Sichuan chilli bean sauce.

Per portion Energy 137kcal/565kJ; Protein 3g; Carbohydrate 5g, of which sugars 4g; Fat 12g, of which saturates 2g; Cholesterol 0mg; Calcium 42mg; Fibre 3g; Sodium 95mg.

Serves 4

450g/1lb/2 cups beansprouts
15ml/1 tbsp vegetable oil
3 garlic cloves, crushed
2 spring onions (scallions),
  cut into 5cm/2in lengths
2.5ml/½ tsp salt

Variation Beansprouts are grown from soaked mung beans. If you can find soy beansprouts, which have larger heads and slightly thicker sprouts, they can be used in this dish.

Per portion Energy 73kcal/303kJ; Protein 42g; Carbohydrate 5g, of which sugars 3g; Fat 4g, of which saturates 1g; Cholesterol 0mg; Calcium 30mg; Fibre 6g; Sodium 252mg.

Stir-fried beansprouts

Of all stir-fried vegetable dishes, this is truly the most universal one. Although of peasant origins, it has transcended all social barriers and is now ensconced in every Chinese home and restaurant around the world. The beansprouts are usually given a hint of salt or soy sauce, and include aromatics like garlic, spring onion, ginger and, sometimes, chillies. Beansprouts have a short shelf life, so choose those that are crisp and firm, and avoid them if they look waterlogged. If they are slightly limp, soak them in ice-cold water for 20 minutes to revive their crispness.

1 Wash the beansprouts and discard any wispy roots or green bean husks. Heat the oil in a wok, add the garlic, and stir-fry for 2 minutes. Add the beansprouts and toss to coat.

2 Stir-fry over high heat for 2 minutes, then add the spring onions and salt. Stir-fry for 30 seconds and serve immediately.

Braised bamboo shoots

In China, most restaurant chefs and home cooks will invariably use fresh bamboo shoots, as they are readily available. Many rural homes will have a patch for growing bamboo. When the shoots are mature, they are pulled up, the outer husks are removed, and the shoots are boiled. This can take several hours. Thankfully, canned bamboo shoots are universally available outside of China, either as whole shoots or sliced into chunks or strips. For this Henan dish, use the whole canned shoots so that you can cut them to any shape or size you like. They have already been processed and boiled, so the cooking time will not be lengthy.

1 Cut the bamboo shoots into bitesize chunks (or slices, if you prefer) and soak them in cold water for 30 minutes. This will reduce the scent and taste of the pickling liquid from the canned shoots.

2 Heat the oil in a wok, add the garlic, and stir-fry for 2 minutes. Drain the bamboo shoots and add them to the pan. Stir-fry for 2 minutes, then add the spring onions.

3 Cook, stirring, for 1 minute, then add the yellow bean sauce, hoisin sauce, sugar, sesame oil, black pepper and 450ml/³⁄₄ pint/2 cups water.

4 Bring to the boil, and simmer over a high heat for 5 minutes. Reduce the heat to medium, and simmer gently for 30 minutes, or until the sauce has reduced by about half. Serve immediately.

Serves 4

450g/1lb canned bamboo shoots
15ml/1 tbsp vegetable oil
2 garlic cloves, crushed
2 spring onions (scallions), chopped
30ml/2 tbsp yellow bean sauce
15ml/1 tbsp hoisin sauce
5ml/1 tsp sugar
30ml/2 tbsp sesame oil
2.5ml/½ tsp ground black pepper

Cook's tip The wonderful thing about bamboo shoots is that no matter how long you cook them, they keep their texture.

Per portion Energy 130kcal/537kJ; Protein 3g; Carbohydrate 4g, of which sugars 3g; Fat 4g, of which saturates 2g; Cholesterol 0mg; Calcium 30mg; Fibre 2g; Sodium 337mg.

Braised tofu

Also known as beancurd, tofu, whether fresh, fried or dried, can be braised with rich or subtle seasonings for a superb vegetarian dish. As a neutral product, tofu absorbs other flavours easily. In China it is not regarded as a meat substitute, but with reverence for its own nutritional and chameleon-like qualities. Using the dried or fried variety will save one step, as you do not need to pre-fry them. They come as squares or cubes with a light brown, slightly wrinkled skin. Use fresh tofu, if you like, but you need to fry it first (see Cook's Tip). With complementary ingredients like mushrooms and vegetables, this dish achieves banquet status.

1 If using dried tofu, cut each square into two triangles. If using fried tofu cubes, you can leave them whole, as they are usually already bitesize.

2 Drain the straw mushrooms. Slice the leek diagonally into 1cm/½in wide slices. Wash in plenty of cold water to remove the soil that often clings to the insides of the white stalks. Drain thoroughly.

3 Heat the oil in a wok, add the leek, and stir-fry for 1 minute. Add the hoisin sauce, dark soy sauce, pepper, wine or sherry, sugar, sesame oil and 350ml/12fl oz/1½ cups water, and bring to the boil.

4 Add the tofu, and simmer for 10 minutes over medium heat. Just before serving, mix the cornflour with a little water and add to the pan. Stir until the sauce thickens a little, then serve immediately, with some plain rice.

Serves 4

350g/12oz dried or fried tofu
115g/4oz canned straw mushrooms
1 leek, white part only
15ml/1 tbsp vegetable oil
30ml/2 tbsp hoisin sauce
15ml/1 tbsp dark soy sauce
2.5ml/½ tsp ground black pepper
15ml/1 tbsp Shaoxing wine
 or dry sherry
2.5ml/½ tsp sugar
15ml/1 tbsp sesame oil
5ml/1 tsp cornflour (cornstarch)
plain boiled rice, to serve

Cook's tip To make your own fried tofu, buy the firm white variety and cut into cubes. Heat plenty of oil until smoking, and deep-fry the tofu, in batches, until a golden skin forms.

Per portion Energy 152kcal/629kJ; Protein 8g; Carbohydrate 3g, of which sugars 1g; Fat 11g, of which saturates 1g; Cholesterol 0mg; Calcium 458mg; Fibre 1g; Sodium 323mg.

Vegetarian stew

A quintessential northern vegetarian dish from Henan, this stew is a signature dish for many Taoist and Buddhist festivals, when meat is not allowed. Most Chinese families, however, serve vegetable dishes as part of every meal, as they demand a good balance of all the food groups. This dish takes a leaf from the eastern Chinese dish Buddha's Vegetarian Stew, which hails from Fujian.

1 Bring 400ml/14fl oz/1⅔ cups water to the boil in a pan, add the black and button mushrooms, and simmer for 10 minutes, or until soft.

2 Remove the mushrooms with a slotted spoon and slice them, then strain and reserve the liquid. Trim off the woody parts from the cloud ear mushrooms.

3 Heat the oil in a wok, add the garlic and ginger, and stir-fry for 2 minutes, then add the preserved red beancurd. Cook, stirring and mashing it a little, for 1 minute.

4 Add the hoisin sauce, salt, pak choi, mangetouts and all the mushrooms. Cook, stirring, for 2 minutes, then add the strained mushroom liquid. Simmer for 15 minutes, or until the sauce is thick. Serve immediately.

Variations
• You can use any mixture of vegetables, but avoid ones that can go mushy, such as squashes, courgettes (zucchini) and marrows (large zucchini).
• Root vegetables and nuts make good additions for extra crunch and nutrition.

Serves 4

4 Chinese black mushrooms
100g/3¾oz button
 (white) mushrooms
40g/1½oz cloud ear (wood ear)
 mushrooms, soaked until soft
30ml/2 tbsp vegetable oil
3 garlic cloves, crushed
25g/1oz fresh root ginger,
 peeled and grated
1 cube preserved red beancurd
30ml/2 tbsp hoisin sauce
5ml/1 tsp salt
200g/7oz pak choi (bok choy),
 sliced into strips
10 mangetouts (snow peas)

Per portion Energy 114kcal/475kJ; Protein 3g; Carbohydrate 7g, of which sugars 1g; Fat 9g, of which saturates 1g; Cholesterol 0mg; Calcium 57mg; Fibre 1g; Sodium 819mg.

Sweet things

In Chinese restaurants outside of China, you may be offered a dessert, but this practice is unheard of in China; sweet dishes are regarded as special treats, afternoon snacks and festive offerings. The range is not large, and the basic ingredients are rice flour, wheat flour, honey, dates, taro and sweet bean paste. Many are an acquired taste, which explains why so few sweet bites are on the menus of takeaways and restaurants outside of China.

Sweet snacks and festive bites

From afternoon snacks to festival food, the tastes and textures of northern Chinese sweet dishes may be a new experience for many people. The fruity, creamy and chocolatey flavours of the West are not found here – intensely sugary morsels are the traditional choices. Many of these are served during festivals and celebrations.

Several types of dates feature in north Chinese sweet dishes and they range from plain, dried ones to cloying honeyed bites. They are often mashed and used as a delicious filling in pancakes.

Apples are often caramelized during festivals, and this is one sweet treat that does appear on menus outside of China. Taro can be given the same treatment, but it is also boiled, mashed and sweetened to make a moreish mouthful.

Sesame seeds, black or white, are used frequently as a crunchy coating for sticky taro slices and steamed glutinous rice.

Although the sweet menu is short, any chef or cook with ingenuity can create their own signature dishes with understanding of the basic ingredients: date pancakes can be tweaked with a dried fruit paste filling, and taro can be replaced by pumpkin or sweet potato for a starchy substitute.

The intense, cloying sweetness might be too much for some palates. Although this is the traditional flavour of authentic Mandarin sweet snacks, you can adjust the amount of sugar to suit your own taste.

Serves 4

75g/3oz/⅔ cup self-raising
 (self-rising) flour
1 egg, lightly beaten
4 large eating apples
vegetable oil, for deep-frying
30ml/2 tbsp vegetable oil
250g/9oz soft dark brown sugar

Variation Banana slices can be
caramelized in the same way.

Caramelized apples

*The origin of this dish is obscure, and it seems to have a higher profile in
Chinese restaurants outside of China than within it. During festival times,
however, children in Beijing can be seen munching the candied fruits, which
are sold on sticks for ease of eating during the festivities. In this recipe,
the apples are cored and cut into pieces for serving on a plate. Chinese
chefs have an ingenious way of caramelizing sugar in a little lard or oil.*

1 To make the batter, sift the flour into a mixing bowl, and stir in the beaten egg. Gradually
add 120ml/4fl oz/½ cup cold water, and stir to make a smooth batter the consistency of
double (heavy) cream. Set aside for 20 minutes. Fill a bowl with iced water, and set aside.

2 Peel and core the apples, and cut each into eight pieces. Heat the oil for deep-frying
in a wok or deep-fryer. Working in batches, quickly dip the apple pieces in the batter,
then deep-fry them for 2–3 minutes, until golden brown. Remove with a slotted spoon,
and drain on kitchen paper.

3 In a separate non-stick wok, heat the 30ml/2 tbsp vegetable oil until smoking, then add the
sugar. Swirl the wok around until the sugar becomes a light brown caramel. Immediately,
add the apple pieces, a couple at a time, and toss them in the caramel with a pair of wooden
spoons. When well coated, lift each piece with a slotted spoon and dunk into the iced water
for a few seconds. You will notice the sugar being pulled into threads. Serve immediately.

Per portion Energy 448kcal/1899kJ; Protein 4g;
Carbohydrate 95g, of which sugars 81g; Fat 9g,
of which saturates 1g; Cholesterol 58mg;
Calcium 116mg; Fibre 4g; Sodium 113mg.

Caramelized taros

Here, taros are cooked rather like Caramelized Apples, but with the addition of sesame seeds to give extra crunch. This is much less sweet than caramelized apples, but equally delicious.

1 Fill a bowl with iced water, and set aside. Wash the taro pieces, and pat them very dry with kitchen paper.

2 Heat the oil for deep-frying in a wok or deep-fryer, and deep-fry the taro pieces, in batches, for about 3 minutes, until cooked through and golden brown.

3 In a clean wok, heat the 15ml/1 tbsp oil and add the sugar. Swirl the wok around until the sugar becomes a light brown caramel.

4 Add the fried taro pieces, in batches, and stir for 1 minute with a pair of wooden spoons. Add the sesame seeds, and stir gently for 1 minute, or until each piece of taro is coated.

5 Lift each piece with a slotted spoon and dunk into iced water. Drain and serve warm.

Variation You can also toast the sesame seeds before using. Spread them out on a foil-lined baking tray, and place under a hot grill (broiler) for a few minutes, until the seeds are a light brown. This will give the finished dish a fragrant, nutty flavour.

Serves 4

450g/1lb taros, cut into
  bitesize pieces
vegetable oil, for deep-frying
15ml/1 tbsp vegetable oil
130g/4½oz/scant ¾ cup caster
  (superfine) sugar
30ml/2 tbsp sesame seeds

Per portion Energy 360kcal/1516kJ; Protein 3g; Carbohydrate 64g, of which sugars 35g; Fat 12g, of which saturates 1g; Cholesterol 0mg; Calcium 82mg; Fibre 4g; Sodium 8mg.

Date pancakes

Two types of Chinese dates are used in cooking: small red, dried dates, which are unsweetened, and black, boiled dates. There is a third, less common, variety called mi zao in Mandarin, which is coated with honey and eaten as a snack, but it is also ideal for making sweet pastries like this Henan date cake. This variety can be hard to find, even within China, so use dried red dates, which are sold in all Chinese stores.

1 Sift the flour into a large bowl and make a well in the centre. Add the egg, and stir to mix. Gradually add 200ml/7fl oz/scant 1 cup water. Stir to make a smooth pouring batter. Set aside.

2 Put the dates into a small pan and add water to just cover. Boil for 10 minutes, or until the dates are completely soft. Drain the dates, reserving the liquid. Remove any skins that might have come away from the dates, and remove the stones (pits).

3 Press the dates through a sieve (strainer), and discard the skins. Using a fork, mash the dates a little more, and add a little of the reserved liquid – enough to make a creamy paste.

4 Heat the lard or white cooking fat in a clean wok and cook the sugar until it is golden brown. Add the date mash, stir well to mix, then remove from the wok and set aside to cool.

5 Heat a small frying pan with a little oil and pour in 30ml/2 tbsp of the batter. Swirl the pan around to create a thin pancake. Cook until the underside is set, then flip it over to cook the other side. Repeat with the remaining batter.

6 Spread 15ml/1 tbsp of the date mash on to each pancake, and fold over to encase the paste. Tuck the loose sides underneath and seal with a little water.

7 In the same pan, add a little more oil and fry each folded pancake for 1 minute on each side. Heat the oil for deep-frying in a wok or deep-fryer, and deep-fry each pancake until bubbly and golden brown. Cut into pieces and serve warm.

Serves 6–8

125g/4¼oz/generous 1 cup plain (all-purpose) flour
1 egg, lightly beaten
vegetable oil, for deep-frying, plus extra for the pancakes

For the filling
175g/6oz Chinese red dates
30ml/2 tbsp lard or white cooking fat
40g/1½oz/3 tbsp caster (superfine) sugar

Variations
• Mediterranean dates can also be used, if you cannot find Chinese red dates. If they are sugar-coated, reduce the sugar quantity by half.
• Sweet pastes made from sesame seeds or almonds can be used for this snack. If you can find the canned pastes, it will save you a lot of time.

Per portion Energy 178kcal/749kJ; Protein 3g; Carbohydrate 24g, of which sugars 12g; Fat 8g, of which saturates 2g; Cholesterol 32mg; Calcium 32mg; Fibre 1g; Sodium 13mg.

Sweet sesame rolls

Sesame seeds come in two types: white or black. This favourite Beijing snack traditionally uses the white type, but you can use either, since, apart from their colour, there is no difference in taste. These look very pretty with a mixture of white and black seeds, as here. The sesame seeds are used to make an outer coating for these rolls, made from glutinous rice with a filling of sweet red bean paste, which is sold in cans in Chinese stores.

1 Wash and rinse the soaked glutinous rice and put it on to a plate that will fit into your steamer. Steam for 30 minutes, or until very soft.

2 Meanwhile, warm the sweet bean paste in a microwave for 1–2 minutes, or until just soft, to make it more manageable. Divide the sweet bean paste into two portions. Divide the cooked rice into two portions.

3 Spread a piece of clear film (plastic wrap) about 15 x 18cm/6 x 7in on to a Japanese bamboo mat for rolling sushi, if you have one, or a piece of baking parchment.

4 Spread the glutinous rice in a layer on the clear film, and top it with the warm sweet bean paste. Spread the paste into an even layer with a moistened butter knife or metal spatula.

5 Roll up like a Swiss roll (jelly roll), using the the mat or baking parchment to help you. Put the sesame seeds on to a large plate. Gently lift the roll and place it on to the sesame seeds. Roll it gently to coat it all over in the seeds.

6 Cut into 2.5cm/1in slices to serve warm. The dish can also be chilled and served cold.

Serves 4

150g/5oz/generous ²/₃ cup glutinous rice, soaked for 3 hours
115g/4oz sweet red bean paste
115g/4oz/1 cup white or black sesame seeds, or a mixture

Cook's tips
• Sweet red bean paste straight from the can is a little stiff, so it helps to heat it in the microwave briefly.
• If not serving immediately, do not keep the rolls warm, as this can cause bacteria to grow in the rice. Allow to cool, then chill.
• A mixture of both white and black sesame seeds gives an attractive monochrome effect, but you can just use one or the other, if you like.

Per portion Energy 351kcal/1463kJ; Protein 9g; Carbohydrate 39g, of which sugars 9g; Fat 17g, of which saturates 2g; Cholesterol 6mg; Calcium 218mg; Fibre 1g; Sodium 126mg.

Taro cream

When it comes to tubers such as taro, potatoes or sweet potatoes, the Chinese do not make a clear distinction between them. They are all regarded as starchy bases and are used in similar ways, though taro is by far the most popular. Taro cream is believed to have originated in the Fujian province, but has since been adopted by chefs of many provinces, particularly in the northern areas. It is sweet, smooth and comforting, and is served as a dessert or snack. You can adjust the amount of sugar to taste, or use a sugar substitute, if you like. This cloying dish is normally served lip-scaldingly hot.

1 Place the taro in a pan, add just enough water to cover, and bring to the boil. Simmer for 25 minutes, then allow to cool. Mash into a smooth paste.

2 Mix the paste with lard or white cooking fat and sugar in a bowl that will fit into your steamer, and cover with a plate or clear film (plastic wrap).

3 Steam for 20 minutes, stirring once or twice, until the sugar has completely dissolved. Serve immediately.

Cook's tip There are two common types of taro, a large tuber about the size of a grapefruit and a smaller one like a plum. Both have white flesh flecked with purple, but the smaller variety has the better flavour.

Serves 4

450g/1lb taro or yam, peeled and
  cut into large chunks
100g/3¾oz lard or white cooking fat
150g/5oz caster (superfine) sugar

Per portion Energy 490kcal/2053kJ; Protein 2g; Carbohydrate 69g, of which sugars 41g; Fat 25g, of which saturates 10g; Cholesterol 23mg; Calcium 32mg; Fibre 4g; Sodium 7mg.

Suppliers

UNITED STATES

The House of Rice Store
3221 North Hayden Road
Scottsdale, AZ 85251
Tel: (480) 947 6698

99 Ranch Market
140 West Valley Boulevard
San Gabriel, CA 91776
Tel: (626) 307 8899

Hong Kong Supermarket
18414 Colima Road
Los Angeles, CA 91748
Tel: (626) 964 1688

Seafood City Supermarket
1340, 3rd Avenue, Chula Vista
San Jose, CA 91911
Tel: (619) 422 7600

Ai Hoa
860 North Hill Street
Los Angeles, CA 90026
Tel: (213) 482 4824

Oriental Grocery
11827 Del Amo Boulevard
Cerritos, CA 90701
Tel: (310) 924 1029

Unimart American and
 Asian Groceries
1201 Howard Street
San Francisco, CA 94103
Tel: (415) 431 0326

Georgia Asian Foods, Etc.
1375 Prince Avenue
Atlanta, GA 30341
Tel: (404) 543 8624

Augusta Market Oriental Foods
2117 Martin Luther King
 Jr. Boulevard
Atlanta, GA 30901
Tel: (706) 722 4988

Hong Tan Oriental Food
2802 Capitol Street
Savannah, GA 31404
Tel: (404) 233 6698

Khanh Tan Oriental Market
4051 Buford Highway NE
Atlanta, GA 30345
Tel: (404) 728 0393

Norcross Oriental Market
6062 Norcross-Tucker Road
Chamblee, GA 30341
Tel: (770) 496 1656

The Oriental Pantry
423 Great Road
Acton, MA 01720
Tel: (978) 264 4576

May's American Oriental
 Market
422 West University Avenue
Saint Paul, MN 55103
Tel: (651) 293 1118

Nevada Asian Market
2513 Stewart Avenue
Las Vegas, NV 89101
Tel: (702) 387 3373

Dynasty Supermarket
68 Elizabeth Street
New York, NY 10013
Tel: (212) 966 4943

Asian Supermarket
109 E. Broadway
New York, NY 10002
Tel: (212) 227 3388

Kam Man Food
 Products
200 Canal Street
New York, NY 10013
Tel: (212) 571 0330

Hang Hing Lee Grocery
33 Catherine Street
New York, NY 10013
Tel: (212) 732 0387

Oriental Market
670 Central Park Avenue
Yonkers, NY 10013
Tel: (212) 349 1979

Asian Foods Ltd
260–280 West Leigh Avenue
Philadelphia, PA 19133
Tel: (215) 291 9500

Golden Foods
 Supermarket
9896 Bellaire Road
Houston, TX 77036
Tel: (713) 772 7882

Welcome Food Centre
9810 Bellaire Boulevard
Houston, TX 77030
Tel: (718) 270 7789

UNITED KINGDOM

Wing Yip
375 Nechells Park Road, Nechells
Birmingham, B7 5NT
Tel: 0121 327 3838

Sing Fat Chinese Supermarket
334 Bradford Street, Digbeth
Birmingham, B5 6ES
Tel: 0121 622 5888

Makkah Oriental Food Store
148–150 Charminster Road
Bournemouth, BH8 8YY
Tel: 01202 777303

Ryelight Chinese Supermarket
48 Preston Street
Brighton, BN1 2HP
Tel: 01273 734954

Wai Yee Hong
Eastgate Oriental City
Eastgate Road, Eastville
Bristol, BS5 6XY
Tel: 0845 873 3388

Wing Yip
544 Purley Way
Croydon, CR0 4NZ
Tel: 0208 688 4880

Hoo Hing Cash & Carry
Lockfield Avenue, Brimsdown
Enfield, EN3 7QE

Pat's Chung Ying Chinese
 Supermarket
199–201 Leith Walk
Edinburgh, EH6 8NX
Tel: 0131 554 0358

See Woo
Unit 5, The Point, 29 Saracen Street
Glasgow, G22 5H7
Tel: 0845 0788 818

Chung Ying Supermarket
254 Dobbies Loan
Glasgow, G4 OHS
Tel: 0141 333 0333

Rum Wong Supermarket
London Road
Guildford, GU1 2AF
Tel: 01483 451568

Seasoned Pioneers Ltd
101 Summers Road
Brunswick Business Park
Liverpool, L3 4BJ
Tel: 0151 709 9330

Loon Fung Supermarket
42–44 Gerrard Street
London, W1V 7LP
Tel: 0207 373 8305

New Loon Moon
 Supermarket
9a Gerrard Street
London, W1D 5PP
Tel: 0207 734 3887

Golden Gate Grocers
100–102 Shaftesbury Avenue
London, W1D 5EE
Tel: 0207 437 0014

New China Gate
18 Newport Place
London, WC1H 7PR
Tel: 0207 237 8969

New Peking Supermarket
59 Westbourne Grove
London, W2 4UA
Tel: 0207 928 8770

Newport Supermarket
28–29 Newport Court
London, WC2H 7PO
Tel: 0207 437 2386

See Woo Hong
18–20 Lisle Street
London, WC2H 7BA
Tel: 0207 439 8325

Wing Yip
395 Edgware Road
London, NW2 6LN
Tel: 0208 450 0422

Wing Yip
Oldham Road, Ancoats
Manchester, M4 5HU
Tel: 0161 832 3215

Woo Sang Supermarket
19–21 George Street, Chinatown
Manchester, M1 4HE
Tel: 0161 236 4353

Miah, A. and Co
20 Magdalen Street
Norwich, NR3 1HE
Tel: 01603 615395

Hoo Hing Commercial Centre
Freshwater Road
Chadwell Heath
Romford, RM8 1RX
Tel: 0208 548 3636
Website: www.hoohing.com

Wah-Yu Chinese Supermarket
145 High St
Swansea, SA1 1NE
Tel: 01792 650888

Hong Cheong
115 Oxford St
Swansea, SA1 3JJ
Tel: 01792 468411

Fox's Spices (mail order)
Mason's Road
Stratford-upon-Avon, CV37 9NF
Tel: 01789 266420

AUSTRALIA
Duc Hung Long Asian Store
95 The Crescent
Fairfield, NSW 2165
Tel: (02) 9728 1092

Foodtown Thai Kee Supermarket
393–399 Sussex Street
Sydney, NSW 2000
Tel: (02) 9281 2202

Harris Farm Markets
Sydney Markets
Flemongton, NSW 2140
Tel: (02) 9746 2055

Asian Supermarkets Pty Ltd
116 Charters Towers Road
Townsville, QLD 4810
Tel: (07) 4772 3997

Burlington Supermarkets
Chinatown Mall
Fortitude Valley, QLD 4006
Tel: (07) 3216 1828

The Spice and Herb Asian Shop
200 Old Cleveland Road
Capalaba, QLD 4157
Tel: (07) 3245 5300

Western Australia Kongs
 Trading Pty Ltd
8 Kingscote Street
Kewdale, WA 6105
Tel: (08) 9353 3380

NEW ZEALAND
Golden Gate Supermarket &
 Wholesalers Ltd.
8–12 Teed Street, Newmarket
Auckland Tel: (09) 523 3373

Happy Super Market
660 Dominion Road,
Mt Roskill
Auckland Tel: (09) 623 8220

Lim Garden Supermarket Centre
3 Edsel Street, Henderson
Auckland Tel: (09) 835 2599

CANADA
Arirang Oriental Food Store
1324 10 Ave Sw # 30
Calgary, AB, T3C 0J2
Tel: (403) 228 0980

T & T Supermarket
222 Cherry Street
Toronto, ON, M5A 3L2
Tel: (416) 463 8113
Website: www.tnt-supermarket.com
(16 stores across the country)

Marché Hawai
1999 Marcel Laurin, Saint-Laurent
Montreal, QC
Tel: (514) 856 0226

Hing Shing Market
1757 Kingsway, Vancouver, BC
Tel: (604) 873 4938

Star Asian Food Centre
2053 41st Avenue
W Vancouver, BC
Tel: (604) 263 2892

Tin Cheung Market
6414 Victoria Drive
Vancouver, BC
Tel: (604) 322 9237

Western Oriental Market
101–1050 Kingsway
Vancouver, BC
Tel: (604) 876 4711

Wing Sang Meat & Vegetable Market
3755 Main Street
Vancouver, BC
Tel: (604) 879 6866

Index

A

apples: caramelized apples 148
aubergines: cold aubergine salad
   131

B

bamboo shoots
   braised bamboo shoots 139
   chicken and bamboo shoot
      soup 27
   sliced beef and bamboo shoots
      100
beans
   bean paste cakes 115
   fried beans in garlic sauce 136
beansprouts
   Beijing eel noodles 118
   stir-fried beansprouts 137
beef
   beef and mushroom dumplings
      42
   beef cakes 45
   noodles with minced beef 123
   sliced beef and bamboo shoots
      100
Beijing eel noodles 118
bell peppers *see* peppers
black bean sauce 21, 58, 76, 91
boiled peanuts 130
bok choy *see* pak choi
braised bamboo shoots 139
braised chicken and chestnuts 80
braised duck in peppery soy
      sauce 83
braised fish in yellow bean sauce
      60

braised quails 81
braised tofu 140
bread: steamed bread 117
button mushrooms: vegetarian
      stew 143

C

cabbage
   pickled Chinese cabbage 128
   sweet-and-sour cabbage 134
   see also Chinese cabbage
caramelized apples 148
caramelized taros 149
caraway seeds: cumin and
      caraway lamb 97
carp
   carp in ginger and sesame
      sauce 62
   hot-and-sour carp 61
carrots
   Tung-Po mutton 98
   see also green carrots
cassia lamb 95
chestnuts: braised chicken and
      chestnuts 80
chicken
   braised chicken and chestnuts
      80
   chicken and bamboo shoot
      soup 27
   chicken and prawn ball soup 31
   chicken, pea and tomato soup 28
   chicken with hoisin sauce 75
   chicken with walnuts 74
   Kwei-Fei chicken 79
   Mongolian seafood steamboat
      56
   oil-soaked chicken 77
   Phoenix chicken 76
   sesame-coated chicken 37
   smoked chicken 73
   tea-smoked chicken 70
   white fungus soup with chicken
      26
chicken livers: four treasures meat
      106

chilli bean paste 21
chilli paste: fried leeks with hot
      sauce 135
chilli sauce dip 55, 73, 115
chillies: pickled Chinese cabbage
      128
Chinese black mushrooms:
      vegetarian stew 143
Chinese cabbage 17
   cumin and caraway lamb 97
   Mongolian seafood steamboat 56
   noodles with minced beef 123
   pickled Chinese cabbage 128
   see also cabbage
Chinese celery
   little dragon dumplings 38
   lotus leaf dumplings 41
Chinese maltose
   chicken with walnuts 74
   Peking duck 84
chives: mu shu pork 92
cilantro *see* coriander
cloud ear mushrooms
   hot-and-sour carp 61
   mu shu pork 92
   vegetarian stew 143
cod: mock crab cakes 55
cold aubergine salad 131
coriander
   chicken with hoisin sauce 75
   shredded kidneys in wine sauce
      105
   tea-smoked chicken 70
coriander seeds: smoked chicken
      73
crab: prawn and crab wontons 34

crispy fish 64
cucumbers
   braised duck in peppery soy
      sauce 83
   mock crab cakes 55
   oil-soaked chicken 77
   Peking duck 84
   prawn cutlets 53
cumin and caraway lamb 97

D

daikon *see* mooli
dates: date pancakes 150
demerara sugar
   smoked chicken 73
   tea-smoked chicken 70
dim sum 34–45
duck
   braised duck in peppery soy
      sauce 83
   four treasures meat 106
   Peking duck 84
dumplings
   beef and mushroom dumplings
      42
   little dragon dumplings 38
   lotus leaf dumplings 41

E

eels
   Beijing eel noodles 118
   garlic fish 58
egg flower pork *see* mu shu pork
eggplants *see* aubergines
eggs: steamed egg custard 132

F

fish
   braised fish in yellow bean
      sauce 60
   carp in ginger and sesame
      sauce 62
   crispy fish 64
   hot-and-sour carp 61
   mock crab cakes 55
   raw fish salad 51

red cooked fish 65
    steamed fish with ginger 63
    trout in wine sauce 59
fish balls: Mongolian seafood
    steamboat 56
fish cake: Mongolian seafood
    steamboat 56
five-spice: liver in five spices 103
four treasures meat 106
fresh scallops and pak choi 54
fried beans in garlic sauce 136
fried leeks with hot sauce 135
fruit *see* names of individual fruits

G
game 81, 102
garlic
    fried beans in garlic sauce 136
    garlic fish 58
ginger
    carp in ginger and sesame
        sauce 62
    steamed fish with ginger 63
ginkgo nuts: chicken with hoisin
    sauce 75
glutinous rice: sweet sesame rolls
    153
golden needles
    Mongolian seafood steamboat 56
    mu shu pork 92
green beans: fried beans in garlic
    sauce 136
green carrots: raw fish salad 51
grouper: red cooked fish 65

H
halibut: mock crab cakes 55
hoisin sauce: chicken with hoisin
    sauce 75
honey
    chicken with walnuts 74
    Peking duck 84
hot-and-sour carp 61

K
kai lan 17
kidneys
    four treasures meat 106
    shredded kidneys in wine sauce
        105
Kwei-Fei chicken 79

L
lamb
    cassia lamb 95
    cumin and caraway lamb 97
    minced lamb noodles 119
    sour-and-hot lamb soup 33
    stir-fried noodles and lamb 120
    sweet-and-sour lamb 94
    Tung-Po mutton 98
leeks
    braised tofu 140
    fried leeks with hot sauce 135
    Phoenix chicken 76
    red cooked fish 65
    stir-fried noodles and lamb 120
lettuces
    chicken with walnuts 74
    garlic fish 58
    raw fish salad 51
limes: sweet-and-sour cabbage 134
little dragon dumplings 38
liver
    liver in five spices 103
    Mongolian seafood steamboat 56
    see also chicken livers
lotus leaf dumplings 41
lotus seeds
    chicken with hoisin sauce 75
    lotus leaf dumplings 41
lychees: chicken with hoisin sauce
    75

M
Mandarin pancakes 112
    Peking duck 84
mangetouts: vegetarian stew 143
meat 86–107
    see also beef; lamb; pork
minced lamb noodles 119
mock crab cakes 55
Mongolian seafood steamboat 56

monkfish: braised fish in yellow
    bean sauce 60
mooli
    raw fish salad 51
    sour-and-hot lamb soup 33
mu shu pork 92
mullet: steamed fish with ginger
    63
mung bean noodles: Mongolian
    seafood steamboat 56
mung beans: bean paste cakes
    115
mushrooms 18–19
    beef and mushroom dumplings
        42
    braised tofu 140
    Chinese black 143
    cloud ear 19
    garlic fish 58
    hot-and-sour carp 61
    lotus leaf dumplings 41
    mu shu pork 92
    oyster 19
    shiitake 18
    stir-fried venison 102
    straw 19
    vegetarian stew 143
    white fungus 19
    white fungus soup with chicken
        26
mustard greens: steamed fish with
    ginger 63
mutton: Tung-Po mutton 98

N
noodles 118–123
    Beijing eel noodles 118
    minced lamb noodles 119
    Mongolian seafood steamboat
        56
    noodles with minced beef 123
    pork and turnips 91
    stir-fried noodles and lamb 120
    stir-fried venison 102
    tea-smoked chicken 70

O
offal 103, 105, 106
oil-soaked chicken 77
oxtail stew 99
oyster mushrooms 19

P
pak choi
    fresh scallops and pak choi 54
    vegetarian stew 143
pancakes
    date pancakes 150
    Mandarin pancakes 112
peanuts: boiled peanuts 130
peas: chicken, pea and tomato
    soup 28
Peking duck 84
pepper: braised duck in peppery
    soy sauce 83
peppers
    sweet-and-sour prawns 52
    trout in wine sauce 59
Phoenix chicken 76
pickled Chinese cabbage 128
pig's kidneys
    four treasures meat 106
    shredded kidneys in wine sauce
        105
pig's liver
    liver in five spices 103
    Mongolian seafood steamboat
        56
pineapples: oil-soaked chicken
    77
plums
    steamed fish with ginger 63
    sweet-and-sour cabbage 134
pork 19, 87, 88
    four treasures meat 106
    little dragon dumplings 38
    lotus leaf dumplings 41
    mu shu pork 92
    pork and turnips 91
    tofu and minced pork soup 32
pork fat
    bean paste cakes 115
    beef cakes 45

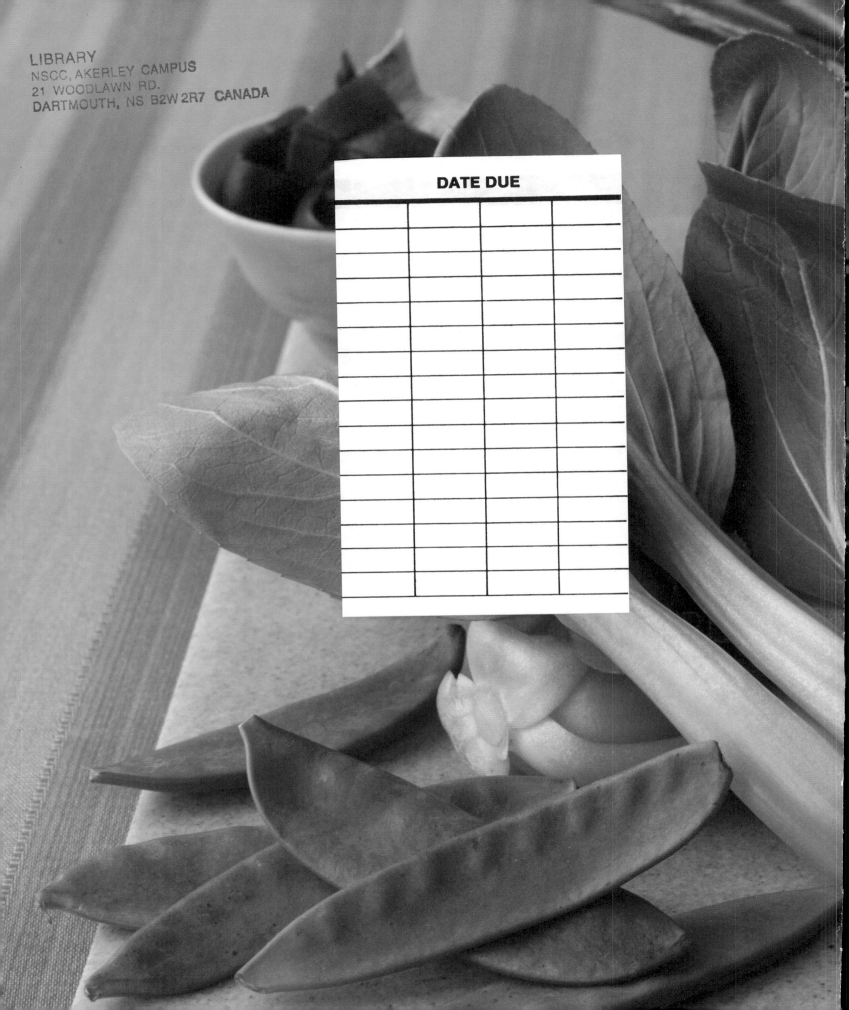

DATE DUE